Dear God,
It's Me and
It's Urgent

EASY PRINT BOOKS

Dear God, It's Me and It's Urgent

Prayers for Every

Season of a Woman's Life

Marion Stroud

DISCOVERY HOUSE

PUBLISHERS®

Feeding the Soul with the Word of God

Discovery House Publishers is affiliated with RBC Ministries, Grand Rapids, Michigan.

Requests for permission to quote from this book should be directed to: Permissions Department, Discovery House Publishers, P.O. Box 3566, Grand Rapids, MI 49501, or contact us by e-mail at permissionsdept@dhp.org

Definitions for asterisked* words can be found in the Glossary at the back of the book.

Biblical quotations are taken from the Authorized Version, Crown copyright; the *Good News Bible* published by The Bible Societies/HarperCollins Publishers Ltd, UK, © American Bible Society 1966, 1971, 1976, 1992; the Holy Bible, New International Version © NIV © 1973, 1978, 1984, by Biblica, Inc.™, used by permission of Zondervan. All rights reserved worldwide. www.zondervan.com; the Revised Standard Version, copyrighted 1946, 1952, © 1971, 1973 by the Division of Christian Education and Ministry of the National Council of the Churches of Christ in the USA and *The Living Bible* © 1971 Tyndale House Publishers.

Library of Congress Cataloging-in-Publication Data
Stroud, Marion.
Dear God, it's me, and it's urgent / Marion Stroud.
  p.   cm.
   Includes bibliographical references.
   ISBN 978-1-57293-755-0
1. Christian women—Prayers and devotions. I. Title. II. Title: Dear God, it is me, and it is urgent.
BV4844.S765   2013   242'.843—dc23

Printed in the United States of America

First printing of this edition in 2013

Contents

A Woman Within

An Appointment with God 12
To Be in Your Presence 15
Beloved. 18
Lifted Up. 21
Body Talk 24
Traveling Light. 27
The Serenity Prayer 30
Summer Shining. 33
Blue Monday 36
Keeping Sunday Special. 39
To Be a Pilgrim 42
Morning Glory. 45
Questions 48
Be Thou My Vision 51
The Whole Armor 54

Wind Beneath My Wings 57
The Lord Is My Shepherd 60
Quiet Day 63
Trust Me 66
Mid-life Crisis 69
Dancing with Life 72

A Woman and Marriage

A Bride's Prayer 76
Appreciation 79
Acceptance with Joy 82
Soul Survivor 85
Freewill 88
Forgiveness 91
Communication Gap 96
Not Wanted Any More 99
Retirement 103
Yet Another Wedding 106
For the Sake of the Children. 109

A Woman and Her Children

I'm Going to Have a Baby. 114
Dedication 117
Tantrums. 120
First Day at School 123
Encouragement 126
Quality Time 129
Teach Us to Pray .132
Help! 135
Guilt Trip 138

Shopping with a Daughter 141
Forgive Me 144
The Prodigal 147
A Daughter's Wedding 150
Entrusted to Him. 153
An Arrow in His Hand 156
Let Nothing Be Wasted. 159
Child Free 164

A Woman at Work

Days of Small Things 170
A Prayer for Ironing. 173
Food, Glorious Food 176
The Interview 179
Stepping Out 182
Labor of Love 185
Just for Today. 188
Whose Responsibility? 191
Reconciled 194
Unwanted 197
Well Dressed 200
Time Trap 203

A Woman Who Cares

The Perfect Friend 208
Hospitality. 211
Listening and Loving 214
At Home Where It's Hardest 217
Foot Washing 220
Heart to Heart 223

Reunion 226
Streetwise. 228
After Chemotherapy 231
You Did It for Me. 234

A Woman Growing Older

Changing Scenes 238
Seasons of Life. 241
Legacy of Love 244
Comfort Zones 247
Keep Me at It 250
Fear Not the Lions 253
Bereavement 256
Burning Still 259
Enlarge My Borders 262

Glossary 265
Notes 266
Bibliography 268

For Shirley and Mary
who prayed this book into being,
and for all those women who struggle
to catch a glimpse of God in their everyday lives.

A Woman Within

It is so easy to feel both small and insignificant, having no purpose in the overall scheme of things. And yet in God's eyes there are no mistakes and no nonentities.
Each life is given at just the right time to do and to be something special and irreplaceable. For you and I are lovingly shaped to be the building blocks from which history is created.

An Appointment with God

Don't pray when you feel like it. Have an appointment with the Lord and keep it. A woman is powerful on her knees. **Corrie ten Boom**

Praying gives sense, brings wisdom, broadens and strengthens the mind. Thought is not only brightened and clarified in prayer, but thought is born in prayer. We can learn more in an hour praying than from many hours in studying . . . . God looks at us in love and would have us share in his good work. So he moves us to pray for what he wants to do. **Julian of Norwich**

Dear Lord, I want to thank you
for the privilege of prayer.
Thank you that I can come to you
at any time,
day or night
and know
that you will never be too busy,
too tired
or too concerned
with your own pressing problems—
as even the best of human confidants can be—
to listen
and to care.

But Lord while being thankful
for the privilege,
I do get puzzled
about the process of prayer;
and wonder if I am asking
for the right things
for all the people
who populate my life;
knowing that there are prayers I pray
month after month,
year after year,
and still do not see
the longed for change
within myself and others.

But even though I do not understand
the way you work
in answer to my prayers,
I praise you that no prayer is lost,
ignored, forgotten,
and as I pray
you move
often in hidden, silent ways
to bring about your purposes
which may not be
the thing I asked for in the first place
but which will always
  work out
for my good
if I will trust you.

Executives are hard to see
Their costly time I may not waste
I make appointments nervously
And talk to them in haste.
But any time of night or day
In places suitable or odd
I seek and get without delay
An interview with God.

Mark Porter[1]

To Be in Your Presence

O the joys of those who . . . delight in doing every-thing God wants them to, and day and night are always meditating on his laws and thinking about ways to follow him more closely. They are like trees along a river bank bearing luscious fruit each sea-son without fail and all they do shall prosper.

Psalm 1:1–3, TLB

If we hope to move beyond the superficialities of our culture—including our religious culture—we must be willing to go down into the recreating silences, into the inner world of contemplation.

Richard Foster

Sometimes, Lord, I really have to wonder
what would have happened
if Martha had joined Mary
in simply sitting at your feet.
Would all the other people there
have inwardly complained
or even had a word with Lazarus
about the standard
of his hospitality?

I sense I'm basically a Martha, Lord,
which means I've got a lot to learn from Mary.
I find it so much easier

to bustle around
and do the things that scream for my attention
than to sit here
trying to relax my body,
still my clamorous thoughts
and simply pay attention
to your voice.

I am so very prone, Lord,
to rush into your presence,
cast my eye fleetingly
over the "passage of the day"
and then present you
with a list of my requests.
Forgive me, Lord.
I know that that's no way
to treat the lover of my soul.

So slow me down please, Lord.
Reassure me
that it is perfectly all right
for me to "waste time" in your presence,
without assessing in what way
or even whether this kind of prayer
has positive results
or brings rewards.
That you are pleased
when I'm prepared to lavish
my time and my attention
on you alone.

Here I am Lord, open
to anything you want to say or show me.
And as I make myself available to you
as best as I know how,
please meet with me,
for Lord you know
I long to meet with you.

To be in your presence,
    To sit at your feet
Where your love surrounds me
    And makes me complete
This is my desire O Lord
    This is my desire.
This is my desire O Lord
    This is my desire.

Noel Richards[2]

Beloved

You are my dearest [daughter],
    the one I love best.
Whenever I mention your name,
    I think of you with love.
My heart goes out to you.

Jeremiah 31:20, GNB

It was I who taught [you] to walk,
    taking [you] by the arms;
I drew [you] to me with affection and love.
I picked [you] up and held [you] to my cheek;
I lifted the yoke from [your] neck
    and bent down to feed [you].

Hosea 11:3–4, GNB; NIV

Father, sometimes I find it very hard
to take hold of the fact
that I am your beloved.
It's difficult to grasp,
when I am still so very much aware
of all the flaws,
that when you look at me
you simply see
someone that you have chosen
to call your child.
Utterly forgiven.
Totally accepted.

Infinitely loved.

And Father, thank you that I have no need
to try and hide
the way I am deep down;
those thoughts and actions
of which I am ashamed.
For you, dear Father, know me through and
through
and nothing
that I or anybody else
can say about me
will ever catch you unawares.
Only with you
can I know ultimate security
because you know the best
and the worst about me
and love me just the same.

Just as I feel the sun, pouring down
out of a summer sky
warming the air
and bringing color and life
to all it touches,
help me to feel and understand
more of the wonder
of this undeserved,
unconditional,
life-transforming
love.
To grasp the fact

that even I can bring you joy,
and most of all
enable me to love you, as I long to,
in return.

God has chosen you out of all the peoples
on the face of the earth to be his people, his
treasured possession.

Deuteronomy 7:6, NIV

The mountains and hills may crumble,
but my love for you will never end.

Isaiah 54:10, GNB

Lifted Up

The Lord is faithful to all his promises
    and loving towards all he has made.
The Lord upholds all those who fall
    and lifts up all who are bowed down.

Psalm 145:13–14, NIV

I have noticed that in every age God has appointed some to say, "There is a lifting up." Their lives say it. They live in the world, buffeted by the problems of the world, and yet not cast down by them. Their very presence, the light in their eyes, and the tone of their voice says, "There is a lifting up."

Amy Carmichael[3]

Dear God,
The impossibility factor
seems to be sky high today.

You know just what the night was like, Lord.
My whole being crying out
for rest, for peace
and just a little moment of forgetting.
But instead of sleep
came endless hours—or so it seemed, Lord—
of tossing and turning,
while my thoughts
went round and round

like a hamster on a wheel,
ceaselessly rehearsing
the problems and pressures
of the week that lies ahead.

And now that morning's here at last, Lord,
I feel both thankful—
because I can get up and *do* something—
and terrified because I don't know *what* to do.
Even the weather sighs and weeps with me,
and my spirit is as low as the mercury
on that depression-sensitive barometer.
My body aches,
my stomach churns
and my mind refuses to grapple any longer
with the plans that I must make.

There seems to be no way out, or over or
    round . . .
I can't cope with the time scale
in which these tasks must be done,
the people with whom I have to do them,
and most of all, Lord, I can't cope with myself.
If ever I needed help I need it now.

You said,
"Come to me, all you who are weary and
    burdened,
and I will give you rest."
I come to you now.

You said, "Do not worry about tomorrow . . .
your father in heaven knows . . ."
and so I just bring you my today.
You said, "If you have faith . . . nothing will be
impossible . . ."
I ask for that faith which is your gift, Lord.

Please lift my eyes from my circumstances to
   your
certainties;
from my weakness to your strength;
from my impossibilities
to your endless capacity to meet every need.

And thank you that you not only lift me up,
but keep me on my feet,
when I share the yoke and the burden with you.

Leave all your worries with him, because he
cares for you.

1 Peter 5:7, GNB

Body Talk

Do you not know that your body is a temple of the Holy Spirit? . . . Therefore honor God with your body.   **1 Corinthians 6:19–20, NIV**

I can do anything I want to if Christ has not said no, but some of these things aren't good for me. Even if I am allowed to do them, I'll refuse to if I think that they might get such a grip on me that I can't easily stop when I want to. For instance, take the matter of eating. God has given us an appetite for food and stomachs to digest it. But that doesn't mean that we should eat more than we should.   **1 Corinthians 6:12–13, TLB**

Dear God, I know I need to lose some weight.
The mirror tells me so,
my clothes all tell me so—
especially the ones
without elastic waists.
Even my doctor mentions
that extra pounds
can predispose my body
to all manner
of unpleasant ailments.

Dear God, I know I need to lose some weight,
but it's so hard

to feed a hungry family
while counting calories as well as cost.
And then there's entertaining, God.
The Bible tells us that hospitality
is a way that we can show your love
and it's a form of relaxation
and celebration
that I enjoy.
And mixed with all these good
    excuses, God,
I must admit that I feel guilty.
Guilty because I turn to food
for comfort and support when life is
    stressful
instead of you.
Guilty because so many people in
    the world
have far too little
while we within the West have far
    too much.
And guilty because I lack the discipline
to exercise more
while eating less.

Please help me, God.
Help me to face the fact that I have
    choices,
and forgive me for abusing
this body that you have given.
For when I pause to think about it

I know that I am
fearfully and wonderfully made.
Help me to love my body enough
to want to keep it fit
and agile and active—
yes, and attractive Lord.
And help me to be obedient to
   your prompting
to take myself in hand,
and with your help,
to lose some weight.

I do not surrender to the temptations of the flesh, for I am not, nor will I become a slave to the flesh. Rather I choose to obey God. I choose the way of righteous obedience. Here I am, Father, what would you have me to do?

Romans 6:16, paraphrased

Traveling Light

Jesus replied . . . "Watch out! Be on your guard against all kinds of greed; a man's life does not consist in the abundance of his possessions."

Luke 12:15, NIV

It was a nightmare! The conference was over and as I returned to my room to pack, I realized that my belongings had multiplied so that I could no longer cram them into two suitcases. Searching frantically for a third bag, it dawned on me that I only had two hands! As I struggled, sweating, out of the mists of sleep, God spoke very clearly: "Dump the cases," He said. "All you need is a backpack."

Please help me to unclutter my life, Lord.
It's not just domesticity
that seems to be getting
completely out of hand,
although when that avalanche
of empty margarine tubs
fell out of the cupboard
and onto my head,
I got the message
that some ruthless weeding out
is needed in that department.

You said that no man—or woman—
can serve two masters,
but Lord, there seem to be
far more than two masters
demanding attention
in my life.
People, commitments, activities, work. . . .
How can I unclutter my life
without being unkind
or seeming uncaring?

You know, Lord, that I sometimes think
I need to fast,
not just from food,
but from excess in every area of my life.
The social occasions I attend
with little pleasure
because it's possible
they'll be of use for networking.
I really do need to abstain
from borrowing a multiplicity of
   library books
just in case
the extra ones that catch my eye
might have been borrowed
next time I come;
and videoing television programs
that I know
I won't have time to watch.

And while I'm at it Lord, please help me
to unclutter my mind
of past hurts, resentments or regrets
of self blame and accusation.
Give me focus and serenity,
enabling me
to embrace the discipline of simplicity
with joy,
as I travel light
in every area of my life.

Empty-handed
    that is how he wanted me.
He commanded
    I lay down my own plans at his feet
        till I had nothing
            nothing of my own,
And then he filled my life
        to overflowing.

John Pantry[4]

The Serenity Prayer

Teach me, Lord, what you want me to do,
and lead me along a safe path.

Psalm 27:11, GNB

God grant me the serenity to accept the things I
cannot change, the courage to change the things
I can, and the wisdom to know the difference.

Dear Lord, I often try to pray for others,
but today it's me—
not my husband or my children
or even my friends—
who stands in need
of an audience with you.

You look at me and see the turmoil, Lord.
The endless questions
going round and round
inside my head.
It seems impossible to stay
the least bit calm or trusting
when all around me
is heading for disaster.
Only you can give me the capacity
to stay unruffled
within the center
of the storm.

Everything that is within me, Lord,
wants to rise up
and yet again
to try and take this situation by the throat;
forcing things
and people into line,
even though I know
that that's impossible.
Please help me to accept that fact
with grace and cheerfulness,
setting to work
upon the blind spots in my own life
before I start to criticize
those in other people.

But there are things
that are within my orbit
where I can make a difference.
Please show me what these are
and give me the courage, Lord,
to get to grips
with issues that may make me
less than popular
with those whose good opinion I still value;
discerning the difference
between doing the thing that pleases you
and that which simply panders
to my opinion
of how the world should be.

All heaven is waiting to help those who will discover the will of God and do it.

J. Robert Ashcroft

Let each look to himself and see what God wants of him and attend to this leaving all else alone.

Henry Suso

Summer Shining

Shine like stars . . . as you hold out the word of
life.   **Philippians 2:15–16, NIV**

I saw a human life ablaze with God,
   I felt a power divine
As through an empty vessel of frail clay
   I saw God's glory shine.

Then woke I from a dream and cried aloud
   "My Father give to me
The blessing of a life consumed by God
   That I may live for thee."

Amy Carmichael

Thank you, Lord, for shining summer days,
when all my life
is bright and sun-kissed,
and I can take the time
to walk more slowly,
look more carefully,
listen more intently,
and anything seems possible.
Thank you for the sunshine's power
to color, cheer, and nurture life
in this fantastic world
that you have made.

Thank you for the sunshine of your love, Lord,
that warms my heart

and brings me joy and peace,
regardless of the season.
Although I must confess
there are occasions
when I'd prefer
to draw the curtains of my life,
exclude the light
that gives both life and comfort;
because I know that it will also show
the dusty corners and the dirt
that in the darkness
can molder quietly,
safely undetected.

Thank you, Lord, that even in the wider world
your light still shines
regardless of the fact
that folk in general may seem oblivious.
So I would dare to pray, dear Lord,
that you won't merely shine on me
but shine through me;
and even though I hesitate to ask it—
knowing myself
and all the times that I fall short—
that you will set my life ablaze.

For only then is there the slightest chance
that I will shine
just like a hilltop city
or warning beacon
to bring to those with whom I live,

who often seem to stumble onward
confused and in despair,
a gleam of hope
that there's a better way.

You are like light for the whole world. . . . Your
light must shine before people so that they will
see the good things you do and praise your
Father in heaven.

Matthew 5:14–15, GNB

Blue Monday

Praise the Lord, my soul
    and do not forget how kind he is
He forgives all my sins
    and heals all my diseases.
He keeps me from the grave
    and blesses me with love and mercy.
He fills my life with good things,
    so that I stay young and strong like an
    eagle.

Psalm 103:2–5, GNB

Dear Lord, I seem to have awoken
yet again
with what my grandmother called
a "black dog"
on my shoulder.
Actually Lord,
a black dog would probably be
a better companion
than this grey fog
which wraps itself around my spirits
with dulling tentacles of dank despair.

If there was some great problem in my life
I could excuse it, Lord.
But there is nothing that is not the common lot
of man—or woman.

There is no obvious reason
to feel this nagging discontent
about the state of my hormones,
my health, my house,
my job, my face, my figure,
my friendships, my family, my finances
and most of all my future, Lord.
On days like this I really wonder
if there is one.
And then I feel so guilty Lord,
because there are so many women
who have real cause
to be in pain
about so many of these features
of the fabric of our lives.

There is a time for grief and tears, Lord.
And when those times occur
I know that I can bring
the darkness to your feet,
and that you'll comfort then,
without reproach.
But in the steady march of each day's journey,
please free me from this habit
of seeing the negatives
rather than the positives
in every situation.

Change my focus, Lord.
Open my eyes to the abundance
of simple joys

and daily mercies
that you have placed within my reach.
And on this day, Lord,
burn through the fog of my depression
and brand my heart
with an attitude of gratitude.

Focus today on the little touches of God's hand
that you would normally take for granted; grasp
the beauty of the moment. If you have to cook
a meal, pause briefly before you begin and give
thanks for the privilege of providing nourishment
and enjoyment for others, and that you have the
resources and opportunity to do so. When you
apply enthusiasm and thanksgiving to any job,
that job comes alive with exciting possibilities.

Keeping Sunday Special

The Sabbath is the golden clasp that binds together the volume of the week.

Observe the Sabbath and keep it holy. You have six days in which to do your work, but the seventh is a day of rest dedicated to me.

Exodus 20:8–9, GNB

Some Pharisees wanted a reason to accuse Jesus of doing wrong, so they watched him closely to see if he would heal on the Sabbath.... Jesus said to them, "...What does our Law allow us to do on the Sabbath? To help or to harm? To save a man's life or destroy it?" **Luke 6:7, GNB**

Just for once, Lord, I've been woken
by the sound of bells
chiming their message
that on this day
you call your people to meet with you
and one another.

When I was a child, Lord, many people
would have obeyed that summons.
The shops would have been shut,
the roads quiet,
the parks empty.

For Sunday was a different day,
not universally enjoyed perhaps
by youngsters who found "Sunday best,"
long sermons and restricted play-time irksome,
but nonetheless a day
when there was opportunity
to pause and recharge batteries
run down by all the pressures of the week.
But now, Lord, what has happened
to keeping "Sunday special"?
The shops are open, car-boot sales* are full,
and sporting events make demands
on time and travel and togetherness.
We've lost the boundaries
of custom and of law
which help to set an atmosphere
of quiet and rest.
So even those of us who want to pause
and spend some time with you
are tempted, once we've been to church,
to treat the first day of the week
like any other.

We cannot legislate for others, Lord,
but will you help us
to see how we can stem the tide
of busyness within ourselves.
To have the discipline to finish jobs
during the week
and come to worship you

with hearts prepared to hear your voice.
Help us to be creative and find ways
to rediscover quietness and freedom
from the demands of ordinary life.
So that on this, your day,
we're both renewed and truly re-created
from the inside out.

If my private world is in order, it will be because
I have chosen to press Sabbath peace into the
rush and routine of my daily life, in order to find
the rest that God prescribed for Himself and all
of humanity.

Gordon MacDonald[5]

Sunday clears away the rust of the whole week.

Joseph Addison

To Be a Pilgrim

Blessed are those whose strength is in you,
who have set their hearts on pilgrimage. . . .
They go from strength to strength,
till each appears before God in Zion.

Psalm 84:5, 7, NIV

As the time approached for him to be taken up to
heaven, Jesus resolutely set out for Jerusalem.

Luke 9:51, NIV

Father, you know that I've been reading
of some of the ancient founders of our faith,
and about those who have made pilgrimage
to places where they lived,
and where it seems
that there is thought to be
a tangible impression
of holiness and you.

Father, I would love to be
a pilgrim.
Abandoning concerns of everyday,
both large and small,
and setting out on an adventure
in company of those who love your name.
I know that pilgrimages in ancient times
were difficult and often dangerous;

that those who went on them
had to be prepared for enemies to bar their path
and to keep alert for danger and attack.
But they had joy in traveling together;
in seeing you provide
their needs along the way.
They could endure
the hardships and the problems,
counting them to be
of small importance
because they were quite confident
about the value
of their pilgrimage
and certain of their final destination.

So, Father, I would pray
for all your children.
For all of us are on a journey,
whether or not we're free
to travel
to sacred places.
Give us a sense of purpose,
a vision
of where we're going and why.
Help us to love and value
our fellow pilgrims,
And keep our destination
in the forefront of our minds;
as together we move steadily
towards the light.

We are the pilgrims, Master;
   we shall go
   Always a little further; it may be
Beyond the last blue mountain
   barred with snow
   Across that angry or that
   glimmering sea.

James Flecker

There's no discouragement
   will make him once relent
   his first avowed intent
      to be a pilgrim.

John Bunyan

Morning Glory

Every morning a new world is born;
Every day a new chance.

Awake, my soul!
   Awake, harp and lyre!
   I will awaken the dawn.
I will praise you, O Lord,
   among the nations;
   I will sing of you among the peoples.
For great is your love,
   reaching to the heavens;
   your faithfulness reaches to the skies.

Psalm 57:8–10, NIV

Dear Lord, it's very early
but I am wide awake,
dragged ruthlessly from slumber
by a large and noisy crow,
grating out his raucous greeting
to the day.

And what a day
you offer us today, Lord!
Blue-washed sky, tinged apricot and gold,
grass spattered silver,
the May tree, just for these few days
festooned with pink.
All this beauty,

prepared with silent love
and lavished on a sleeping world
though there will be so few
who're wide awake enough
to know or care.

As I open my physical eyes
to the daylight, Lord,
help me to open my heart
to all of your creation.
Let me sense where you're
　　at work
in the people I meet,
and in the situations
in which I find myself.

And today
keep me from passing by uncaringly
any whom I could help or encourage.
Help me not to overlook
ways in which you can speak to me
or guide me.
Keep me from missing
the moments in which you want to deepen
my understanding
of myself and others.

And like that crow, Lord,
proclaiming his message to an oblivious world,
may my life shout out
in word and action

the message of your love,
today and every day.

If you have never heard the mountains singing or seen the trees . . . clapping their hands, do not think that because of that they don't. Ask God to open your ears so that you may hear it and open your eyes so that you may see it, because though few men ever know it, they do my friend, they do.

McCandlish Phillips

Teach me my God and King
in all things thee to see
And what I do in anything
to do it as for thee.

George Herbert

Questions

How long will you forget me, Lord? Forever?
  How long will you look the other way when
  I am in need?
How long must I be hiding daily anguish in
  my heart?
  How long shall my enemy have the upper
  hand?
Answer me, O Lord my God;
  give me light in my darkness lest I die.

Psalm 13:1–3, TLB

In sorrow and suffering, go straight to God with
confidence, and you will be strengthened, enlight-
ened, and instructed.

St. John of the Cross

Today, dear Lord, my head is full
of questions.
Why do you permit this pain?
How long do you expect me to endure?
What possible purpose
can it fulfill in my life,
and in the lives of those I love?

Have you forgotten
the promises you made?
Did I mistake

your guidance?
Why don't you answer
the prayers that I have prayed
over and over?
Is it because I've fallen
too far short
ever to be blessed again?

Why don't you
make him trust you?
Stop her harming herself . . .
and others?
Provide the home,
the job,
the friends
that they so obviously need?
Lord, those are the questions.
Do you have anything to say?

"Faith, my child,
is holding onto me
in the darkness.
Standing firm
when there appear to be
no immediate solutions.
Believing that I am at work
even though you cannot see
things happening.
Will you trust me
like that?"

Don't fret or worry. Instead of worrying, pray.
Let petitions and praises shape your worries
into prayers, letting God know your concerns.
Before you know it, a sense of God's wholeness,
everything coming together for good, will
come and settle you down. It's wonderful what
happens when Christ displaces worry at the
center of your life.

Philippians 4:6–7,
The Message

Anxiety is not only a pain which we must ask
God to assuage, but a weakness that we must
ask him to pardon—for he has told us to take no
care for the morrow.

C. S. Lewis

Be Thou My Vision

We see Jesus . . . now crowned with glory and honor.

Be thou my vision,
   O Lord of my heart.
Naught be all else to me
   Save that thou art;
Thou my best thought
   By day or by night,
Waking or sleeping,
   Thy presence my light.

Riches I heed not,
   Nor man's empty praise,
Thou mine inheritance
   Now and always;
Thou, and thou only,
   First in my heart,
High King of heaven
   My treasure thou art.

St. Patrick

Dear Lord,
will you renew my vision?
Not of the work
that you are calling me
to do for you,

but a vision
of yourself—
the one who does the calling.

Sometimes, Lord,
I feel afraid of what might happen
if I were to see you
in the revelation fullness
of your all-consuming
power and glory.
For surely
I could not look at you like that
and live.
But I do dare to ask, Lord,
to see you more clearly
as loving, tireless Father,
patient, seeking shepherd,
wise and ever-available counselor,
radical leader,
inspiring teacher,
committed friend,
and utterly forgiving Savior.

Help me to seek you for yourself,
not for any benefits
that I might gain
from finding you.
And as I see you
with ever greater clarity,
may I love you more dearly,
and follow you more nearly,

so that any work that I may do for you
will simply be an overflow
of gratitude and praise.

How is your beloved better than others? . . .
My lover is radiant. . . outstanding among ten
thousand. . . .
He is altogether lovely.
This is my lover, this is my friend.

Song of Songs 5:9, 10, 16, NIV

The Whole Armor

Finally, be strong in the Lord and in his mighty power. Put on the full armor of God so that you can take your stand against the devil's schemes.

Ephesians 6:10–11, NIV

Thank you, Lord, that you provide
this belt of truth.
Please help me to discern
the half truths and the lies
hurled at me by the enemy.
And when they scream for entry
at the doorway of my mind,
help me to refuse
both to receive them or believe them.

Thank you for the breastplate
that protects my heart
and my emotions.
Keeping me from being wounded
by the jibes of others,
or being bound
by fear of the reactions
of those whose good opinion
is so important to me.
Banish compromise please Lord,

enabling me
to do what's right—consistently.

And as I wear these running shoes
of the readiness to share your love,
keep me from being sidetracked, Lord,
or from avoiding the stony paths.
Help me to be ready
to go wherever you may send me,
and prepared to set out
at a moment's notice.

I'm grateful, Lord,
that with the shield of faith
I have protection
from head to toe.
No flaming arrows
of doubt or of despair
can pierce my heart
while it is in position.
I'll operate by faith
in what God said
and not in outward situations.

Thank you, Lord,
that with the helmet
of your salvation
comes freedom from old thoughts
and habit patterns.
That you renew my mind, transform it
as I allow your Word

to shape my life,
infusing everything
I do or say or write.

So keep me standing, Lord,
alert and prayerful.
Rejoicing in the fact that
the battle
is already won.

Stand . . . and see this great thing the Lord is
about to do before your eyes!

1 Samuel 12:16, NIV

Wind Beneath My Wings

[The Lord] shielded him and cared for him;
he guarded him as the apple of his eye,
like an eagle that stirs up its nest
and hovers over its young,
that spreads its wings to catch them
and carries them on its pinions.
The Lord alone led him;
no foreign god was with him.

Deuteronomy 32:10–12, NIV

You yourselves have seen what I did to Egypt, and
how I carried you on eagles' wings and brought
you to myself.   **Exodus 19:4, NIV**

Dear Lord, you know
that this has been a weary week,
when I have not responded well
to challenges
that you have placed before me.
Just like a stubborn fledgling,
I've clung to what appears to be
safe and secure;
afraid to leave the nest
in case my faith wings
are too weak
and I crash downward
to the rocks below.

But thank you, Lord,
for word pictures of eagles;
for showing me
that anywhere I have to fly
you're always there.
That you will be
beneath, above, around me,
urging me on and upward into freedom
but also ever ready
to carry and support.

So here I am, Lord,
poised upon the edge and waiting,
a little anxious still,
but trusting that I'll soar as I launch out;
because it is not strength
or cleverness
that will support me,
but resting
on the thermals of your grace.
Then in your strength
I know that I can fly
much higher than the eagle
for you will be the wind
beneath my wings.

Come to the edge
We might fall
Come to the edge
It's too high
Come to the edge
And they came
and he pushed
And they flew.

Christopher Logue

The Lord Is My Shepherd

The Lord is my shepherd, I shall not be in want.
   He makes me lie down in green pastures,
He leads me beside quiet waters,
   He restores my soul.
He guides me in the paths of righteousness
   for his own name's sake.
Even though I walk through the valley of the
   shadow of death,
I will fear no evil,
   For you are with me;
Your rod and staff, they comfort me.

You prepare a table before me in the presence
   of my enemies.
You anoint my head with oil; my cup overflows.
Surely goodness and love will follow me all the
   days of my life,
And I will dwell in the house of the Lord forever.

Psalm 23, NIV

Thank you Lord, that you're my shepherd.
And despite all the responsibilities
that lay heavily on my shoulders,
there is someone right beside me
to carry me and care for my concerns.

I praise you that you choose my pasture with
   care,

and even if I am not aware of what my real
   needs are,
you will see to it that those needs are met
and I will lack nothing that it is good for me to
   have.

Often, Lord, I find myself confused
about what the right path might be,
and so I'm grateful that you will lead me
to the destination you have planned.

When circumstances are dark and hard, Lord,
you will never leave me to go through them on
   my own.
And if I'm too tired, too distracted
or even too stubborn to heed your voice,
you'll use your shepherd tools—
circumstances . . . other people . . . even my
   mistakes
to keep me heading in the right direction.

Sometimes, Lord, there seem to be enemies
   on every side
opposing every step I take.
But I can choose whom I will feast with—
the demons of doubt, discouragement and
   despair
or your lavish provision
of love and light and laughter.

I anoint my head with many things, Lord,
but far more important than any beauty aid

is your oil of joy
and of commissioning for future service.

My eternal life does not begin on the day that I
  die.
This forever quality of living
starts as soon as I accept your shepherdly
  authority
and will see me safely through every age and
  stage
into the cascading light and total love that is
  your heaven.

Quiet Day

How can you expect God to speak in that gentle and inward voice which melts the soul, when you are making so much noise with your rapid reflections? Be silent, and God will speak again.

Francois de la Mothe Fénelon

Lord, you know that I have put this day aside
to spend in quietness with you.
And yet, Lord, even as I cross the threshold
of this lovely place,
my mind is thronged with images
of all the things that I have left undone
at home and in the office.

Am I being self-indulgent, Lord?
Presumptuous even,
hoping that you will come
and meet me here?
How will I cope
with all the empty hours that lie ahead,
if that persistent voice inside my head
speaks truth,
and I am not on your agenda?

I can do little more
than offer you my tension, Lord.
And ask that you will still my mind

as I relax my body.
Please take the jigsaw-puzzle pieces
of my fragmented life;
create from them a thing of beauty
and give me harmony and focus.

Thank you for the knowledge
that as I sit quietly in your presence
I do not have to do anything,
say anything,
feel anything.
That just the very act
of offering my day to you
becomes a gift you will receive with joy,
and that the outcome
is in your hands.

I believe that I can trust your Spirit
to show me what I need to confess,
where I need your forgiveness,
whom I need to love.
And if you choose
to say nothing
that I can grasp hold of with my mind,
I shall still leave this place
able to live differently,
because I will do so from a heart
that has been stilled, refreshed, and reminded
that the only life worth living
is the one that is placed
at your disposal.

I do not concern myself with great
    matters
or things too wonderful for me.
But I have stilled and quieted my
    soul.

Psalm 131:1–2, NIV

I am quiet now before the Lord . . .
    as a child who is weaned from
    the breast. . . .
my begging has been stilled.

Psalm 131:2, TLB

Trust Me

How long, O Lord? Will you forget me
  forever?
    How long will you hide your face from me?
How long must I wrestle with my thoughts
    and every day have sorrow in my heart?
How long will my enemy triumph over me?
Look on me and answer, O Lord my God.
    Give light to my eyes, or I will sleep in
  death.   **Psalm 13:1–3, NIV**

What's happening, Lord?
And why is it happening?
I trusted you
and instead of light
there is darkness.
I feel abandoned, betrayed, unloved.
Where are you, Lord?

My child,
I love you more than you will ever know.
You are my chosen one,
my treasured possession
on whom my favor rests.
I have poured many blessings into your life,
but my plan for you
holds good things still to come,
that you have not even begun to imagine.

When my hand seems to break you—
rather than to bless you—
trust me.
What I take apart
I will put together again
and in making you anew
I will make you strong at the broken places.

When I draw you aside,
and speak words
that others do not seem able to hear—
trust me.
If you will give me time
and attention,
I will share with you
the secrets of my heart;
for I long for an ever-deepening relationship
with you.

If I ask you to walk
the path less traveled
and to march to a different drummer
than your companions seem to hear—
trust me.
I have a task for you,
and a task for them.
What is important
is that you each keep your eyes on me
and feed my sheep and lambs as I direct.
I long to use you;
you are all I have.

Jairus . . . fell at Jesus' feet and begged him to come to his home because his twelve-year-old daughter, his only child, was dying. . . . While Jesus was still talking, someone from the leader's house came up and told him, "Your daughter died. No need now to bother the teacher." Jesus overheard and said, "Don't be upset. Just trust me."

Luke 8:41–42, 49–50,
The Message

Mid-life Crisis

[Caleb said], "Look at me! . . . I am still strong enough for war or for anything else. Now then, give me the hill-country that the Lord promised me on that day when my men and I reported. We told you then that . . . giants . . . were there in large walled cities. . . . The Lord will be with me, and I will drive them out."

Joshua 14:11–12, GNB

Is this what they call the "mid-life crisis," Lord?
This feeling
that life must surely have much more to offer
than I've experienced so far;
coupled with a strange reluctance
to go out and get involved in it?

One half of me refuses to accept
that challenge and excitement
are the prerogative
of the young;
after all, Lord, Caleb was eighty-five
when he selected walled cities and giants
for his inheritance!
But the other half whispers seductively,
"Slow down a bit!
It's time that someone else
took on the rough jobs.

You have done your share;
enjoy life,
relax a little."

It is a tempting thought, Lord!
And yet my better self knows all too well
that I could never be completely satisfied
with the soft option.
For since your call
is not just for a few years,
but for life,
the mountain climbed in your glad company
is infinitely preferable
to the self-chosen easy road
which I would have to walk alone.

So re-fire me, Lord.
Give me a fresh vision
of where I am going, and why.
Enable me to see
what your plan is
for this stage of my life,
and help me to give all I've got
in the doing of it.
If you will lead me on,
then surely I will "strive with things impossible
and get the better of them."

Ultimately, we become the people we choose to be. Although we live together, each of us grows alone. What are we willing to exact from ourselves? It's been said that we're all self-made individuals; however only the successful will admit it!

Ted Engstrom

The woods are lovely, dark and deep,
But I have promises to keep
And miles to go before I sleep.

Robert Frost

Dancing with Life

When asked why she was always so cheerful, an old woman replied, "Well, I try to wear each day as a loose garment."

Jesus said, "Are you tired? Worn out? . . . Come to me. . . . Walk with me and work with me—watch how I do it. Learn the unforced rhythms of grace. I won't lay anything heavy or ill fitting on you. Keep company with me and you'll learn how to live freely and lightly."   **Matthew 11:28, *The Message***

Dear Lord, please help me
to wear today
like a loose garment,
so that I dance through its hours
freely,
easily,
comfortably.
Enable me to be
flexible,
ready to move
at your Spirit's prompting,
flowing
with the current of your will,
rather than being dashed on the rocks
of my own tensions and anxieties.

Cut through the cords
that keep me a prisoner,
forcing me
to hang onto life
as I think
that it's supposed to be.
Help me to see you working for good,
bringing opportunities
for spiritual growth
in all that I experience;
whether I perceive it
to be so at first encounter.

Release the rigid restriction
of my demanding
unrealistic things
of others.
And as I reach out in spirit
to join hands
with the people
you bring to me today,
may we move together
in dances of joy
and may our touch
on one another's lives
bring strength and comfort,
freedom and hope.

For you who fear my name, the Sun of Righteousness will rise with healing in his wings. And you will go free, leaping with joy, like calves let out to pasture.

Malachi 4:2, TLB

I am shaken with gladness
My limbs tremble with joy
My heart and the earth
Tremble with happiness;
The ecstasy of life
Is abroad in the world.

Helen Keller

A Woman and Marriage

A marriage . . .
makes of two fractional lives a whole
it gives two purposeless lives a work,
and doubles the strength
of each to perform it;
it gives two questioning natures
a reason for living
and something to live for;
it will give new gladness to the sunshine
a new fragrance to the flowers
a new beauty to the earth
and a new mystery to life.
Mark Twain

A Bride's Prayer

The Lord God said, "It is not good for the man to live alone. I will make a suitable companion to help him." **Genesis 2:18, GNB**

"I take you... to have and to hold, for better, for worse, for richer, for poorer, in sickness and in health." **The Marriage Service, ASB**

Dear God,
The florist's wire and stepladders have gone,
rehearsal's over,
church is quiet and dim;
and now our wedding,
the day that we've looked forward to,
dreamed about, saved for,
and planned in every detail for so long,
is almost here.

Tonight there's nothing more to do than wait.
Wait until the morning comes,
the guests gather
and I walk up the aisle
to stand beside the one
that I love best in all the world.
I should be feeling absolutely blissful God,
and yet. . . .

Stirring amidst the love, the laughter and
 excitement
there is this feeling of unease.

Am I afraid, dear God?
Or is it just that sinking feeling
with which I'm always dogged
when faced with any unfamiliar situation?
For there is no denying, God,
that though we'd like to feel
we know each other
inside out
our marriage cannot help
but be a journey of discovery.

And though most marriages begin, dear God,
with so much love
and such high expectations,
they often seem to dwindle into boredom
or, worse still,
downright dislike.
We want to make our marriage work,
but in the light of cold reality
perhaps we'll need some help
in order to live happily
ever after.

So please will you be with us, God?
Not simply in the church tomorrow
but will you travel with us
day by day and year by year,

giving us
all that we will need
if we're to weather
the sunshine and the storms
we'll surely face.

I take you . . . to love and to cherish. With my body I honor you. All that I am I give to you. All that I have I share with you, within the love of God.

The Marriage Service, ASB

A successful marriage requires a divorce; a divorce from your own self-love.

Paul Frost

Appreciation

The deepest principle in human nature is the craving to be appreciated.   **William James**

> How do I love thee? Let me count the ways.
>   I love thee to the depth and breadth and
>   height
> My soul can reach. . . .
>
> **Elizabeth Barrett Browning**

> How handsome you are, my dearest;
>   how you delight me!
> Like an apple tree among the trees of
>   the forest,
>   so is my dearest compared to other
> men.
>
> **Song of Songs 1:16; 2:3, GNB**

> Why do I find it so hard, Father,
> to tell him how I really feel?
> When I'm alone,
> I think of all the things
> I love about him;
> the crooked smile,
> the look in his eyes
> when he comes home at night;
> his hands,
> so gentle and yet so strong.

I love his sense of humor,
his care for the helpless and needy,
and the way he really listens
to what I have to say.

I have no inhibitions
about talking about him to others.
I talk to the girls at work
about his virtues,
by the hour,
and on the odd occasions
when we have been apart
I find it easy to write
about how much I love him.

And yet when he holds me in his arms
and whispers compliments
into my ear,
all I can say
is, "I love you too."

"I love you!"
It says it all,
and yet it says so little.
I don't understand
where this embarrassment comes from Lord,
but please will you take it away.
Take away my fear of feeling foolish
or of having my words of love
rejected or misunderstood,
and help me to tell him

how attractive I find him.
To give him the appreciation
and encouragement
that we all want.
Let me take my turn
at being the one
who kisses;
giving without wanting to get anything
in return.
Please make my love like yours.

When someone feels secure in knowing they are special, loved, and valued, he or she can cope with separation, time pressures and the demands of others with comparative ease. But if this sense of being important is missing, they are likely to make more and more frantic efforts to secure it, or else sink down into apathy and despair.

Marion Stroud[6]

Acceptance with Joy

I have learned the secret of being content in any and every situation . . . whether living in plenty or in want.   **Philippians 4:12, NIV**

> Will you continue
> to exhaust yourself
> Battering your wings
> Against immovable bars
> Or will you learn
> To live
> Within the confines
> Of your prison
> And find to your surprise
> That you have strength to sing
> Even there?
>
>   **Kathy Keay[7]**

So often, Lord, it's hard to know
when to wrestle with people
and situations
seeking to change them,
and when to accept
that whether I like it or not,
nothing comes into my life
unless you allow it.

Please help me, Lord.

Help me to know in my heart
as well as in my head
that when I have you in my life
I have all that I need.
And that the only person
whom you ask me to change
is myself.

Reassure me, Lord,
that what you choose to provide
at this moment
is all that is necessary
for me to know
contentment and joy
on this day.

I know, Lord, that you are
  not asking
me to live
in unreality.
To pretend that what is hard
and unwelcome
and painful
does not really exist.

But help me, Lord,
to open my hands
with child-like confidence,
and grasp willingly
whatever
you choose to place there,

knowing
that only you can see
the big picture.
And that you will be
neither early nor late
in your giving,
because your clocks
keep perfect time.

These things I plan won't happen right away.
Slowly, steadily, surely, the time approaches
when the vision will be fulfilled. If it seems slow
do not despair, for these things will surely come
to pass. Just be patient! They will not be overdue
a single day.

Habakkuk 2:3, TLB

Soul Survivor

Refrain from anger and turn from wrath; do not fret—it leads only to evil.   **Psalm 37:8, NIV**

Sometimes, Lord, I must admit
that there appears to be
an awful lot
that can give rise to anger,
when you alone among your family
are still committed
to holding onto faith,
however tentative
your grasp may be.

Life can seem unfair
when all the rest walk into church
with smiling Sunday faces,
outwardly compliant partners
and well-behaved children.
There seems to be
so little thought for those of us
who slip into the back row
on our own
week after week,
or rush out
immediately after the Benediction
because the service has run over—again.

It cannot be so hard
to be holy,
when nobody hints to you
that if you were "more spiritual"
or a "better witness"
(which could be interpreted, Lord,
as "a better wife")
then all your problems
would be resolved!

It is so easy, then,
to gather up these "little twigs"
of irritation
or sheer frustration
and slip them into that invisible sack
on your back.
And when you add the bigger logs,
formed from lack of understanding
and mockery at home,
and the pain and disappointment
of prayers
seemingly not answered,
before long
you can be bent almost double
with the ugly weight
of anger
and of bitterness.

But thank you, Lord,
there is a remedy
for backs bowed and broken

by burdens
that are self-inflicted.
For you are always ready
to lift these sins,
along with all the rest,
from anyone who is prepared and willing
to be released.

There is no other god like you, O Lord . . . You
take pleasure in showing us your constant love.
. . . You will trample our sins underfoot and send
them to the bottom of the sea!

Micah 7:18, GNB

Freewill

[Jesus said to the crowds and to His disciples:] "O Jerusalem, Jerusalem, you who kill the prophets and stone those sent to you, how often I have longed to gather your children together, as a hen gathers her chicks under her wings, but you were not willing."

Matthew 23:37, NIV

God never burglarizes the human will. He may long to come in and help, but He will never cross the picket line of our unwillingness.

Dear Lord, you know
that if I could
I would propel my husband bodily,
and force him
kicking, screaming
to your feet;
thrust his reluctant hand in yours,
and then stand back
and watch his hardness melt away,
excuses disappear,
arguments
dwindle into silence,
when he could see you face to face.

But this I cannot do,
and you will not.
For even though you can do everything,
you will not take from any human heart
the awful privilege of choice,
the daunting freedom of self-will,
and so you will not make us love you.
I cannot break the walls he builds,
unstop his deafened ears
nor change his heart,
if he will not allow you access.

But I can be a wife to him,
a heart's companion, lover, friend,
and show your grace
as best I may,
though failing often as I will,
and seek to share your Spirit's fruits,
to be your heart
and hands
and voice.
That in some quiet moment
he will know that you are real,
and choose to love and follow you,
for dimly in another's life
he will have seen you
face to face.

When a man's wife becomes a Christian it's a . . .
threat. Suddenly she has a love relationship with
someone he can't even see. He can't understand
anything she tries to tell him about this new God
she has come to know. All he knows is that she's
in love with somebody else, and he is jealous.

Linda Davis[8]

Be good wives to your husbands, responsive to
their needs. There are husbands who, indifferent
as they are to any words about God, will be
captivated by your life. . . . What matters is not
your outer appearance . . . but your inner
disposition. . . . Be agreeable,
be sympathetic, be loving, be compassionate, be
humble. That goes for all of you, no exceptions.
No retaliation. No sharp-tongued sarcasm.
Instead bless—that's your job, to bless. You'll be
a blessing and also get a blessing.

1 Peter 3:1–9, *The Message*

Forgiveness

Be kind to one another, tenderhearted, forgiving one another, as God in Christ forgave you.

Ephesians 4:32, RSV

Peter came to Jesus and asked, "Lord, if my brother keeps on sinning against me, how many times do I have to forgive him? Seven times?"

"No, not seven times," answered Jesus, "but seventy times seven."　　**Matthew 18:21–22, GNB**

When a couple come to me and want to get married, I always ask them if they have had a real quarrel—not just a casual difference of opinion, but a real fight. Many times they will say: "Oh, no! We love one another."

Then I tell them, "Quarrel first—then I will marry you." The point is, of course, not the quarreling, but the ability to be reconciled to each other. The question is, "Are we able to forgive each other and to give in to each other?"　　**Walter Trobisch**

A fault confessed is more than half amended.

Lord, you know that we have had
the most almighty row.
In fact, I think the whole world knows
or at the very least

our next-door neighbors.
Who would have thought
that trying to decide
how we should spend an unexpected gift
would bring us to the point
of feeling that our marriage
might be over.

How could two people
who really love each other, Lord,
have such a violent disagreement
over the very thing
that was supposed
to bring us joy?
But surely I was right
when I maintained
that we should have a holiday?
For how could anyone believe
that it would be much better
to spend the lot
on a computer,
even if it would be useful
in your work?

But, Lord, I wish that I could bring them back—
those awful things I said.
Flinging the words like knives;
wanting to hurt him
just as much as he hurt me.
I wish I hadn't brought his mother into it
or the mistakes

he's made on earlier occasions.
I wish I hadn't breakfasted in silence
and then gone out to work
without a touch
or loving word.
O Lord, forgive me.

You know that when we've disagreed before
it's taken ages
before we have been ready to admit
that we were wrong.
We have spent days
hiding behind
a wall of icy silence,
creeping out occasionally
to hurl another wave
of angry words.
Invisible missiles
but in their way as deadly
to our health and happiness
as broken bricks and bottles.

O Lord, please help us both
to put things right.
To recognize that it is not
of any great account
which one of us is right
or most to blame.
That in this kind of war
it's probable that we will both
end up as losers.

And that our love and life together
is so much more important
than any sum of money.

Forgiveness saves the expense of anger, the
cost of hatred, the waste of spirits.

Hannah More

Only one petition in the Lord's prayer has any
condition attached to it; it is the petition for
forgiveness.

William Temple

The three words that keep Romeos and Juliets in
glory are not "I love you" but "I am sorry."

Fred Bauer

If we knew that life would end
tomorrow,
would we still waste today on
our quarrels?
If we knew that life would end
tomorrow,
would we keep a tally of wrongs . . .
determined not to be the first
to give in?
If we knew that life would end
tomorrow . . .
but who can say that it will not?

The only time of which we can be
certain is today.
So today I will reach out for
your hand.
Today I will say, "I'm sorry"
and "I love you."

Marion Stroud[9]

A happy marriage is a union of two good
forgivers.

Robert Quillen

Communication Gap

Why am I afraid to tell you who I am? If I tell you who I am, you may not like who I am, and that is all I have.   **John Powell**

Though conversing face to face, their hearts have a thousand miles between them. **Chinese proverb**

I come to you this morning, Lord,
Feeling both confused and anxious
about my husband.
Something is bothering him Lord,
and I cannot begin to fathom
what it is.
When he walked in last night
his face
was wearing that "closed in" look,
like a window
with its curtains drawn.
And all he would say
was that he was tired
and that they had a lot on
at the office.

Why doesn't he talk to me, Lord?
Why won't he share his problems?
Why can't he say
how he feels?

When he is silent like this
my imagination
works overtime.
Is he facing redundancy*
or perhaps some ghastly illness?
Are we in some terrible financial plight;
is he bored with me
or worse still
has he fallen in love
with someone else?

O bless him, Lord,
and lift this burden
from his shoulders,
whatever it may be.
Help me not to pester or to pry
but be prepared to listen
with patience and with love
when he is ready to talk.
And when that happens, Lord,
help me to do it
without criticizing, condemning
or handing out
unwanted advice.

And, Lord, please help us both
to want to be
more trusting and more open
so that one day we'll learn to say
more easily
the things we really feel.

One of the greatest gifts that we can give to anyone is to listen to them; not just to hear what they are saying, but to listen to them with love, aiming to understand the feelings that lie behind the words.

Marion Stroud

Thoughtless words can wound as deeply as any sword, but wisely spoken words can heal.

Proverbs 12:18, GNB

Not Wanted Any More

Because you are not wanted any more
Shut out and thrown upon the heap are you
Forget the famous things you did before!

Condemned, that night, outside your own
  front door
To loiter, terrified of going through,
Because you are not wanted any more.

And as your former colleagues desperately
  claw
Their way to shelter, they will soon come to
Forget the famous things you did before.

A boardroom bomb and dead directors on
  the floor?
So what? It does not matter what you do
Because you are not wanted any more.

Yes send off applications by the score
"No thanks!" (Too old, wrong sex, wrong hue)
Forget the famous things you did before!

What is the point of it the world is straw.
Where are those burning wishes to pursue?
Forget the famous things you did before.
You are not wanted any more.

Peter Jones

Redundant! My friend's husband
has been declared redundant!*
Dear Lord, what a terrible word
that is.

The employers may try to wrap it up
in jargon phrases;
calling it "downsizing,"
"rationalization,"
"redeployment of resources,"
But he knows
that what it really means
is that he is
"inessential,"
"unneeded,"
"unwanted"
and "surplus to requirements."
In other words, Lord,
he simply isn't wanted any more.

He cried, Lord, when he told her.
The only tears that she had seen him shed
in twenty years.
Then he was angry,
now depressed.
Oh help them both.

Help her to encourage and support, Lord,
Without seeming to underplay
the difficulty
of the situation.

Relieve their anxieties
about money,
where they will live,
and what they will do.

Help him to be thankful
that she still has a job,
and that they have at least one income
even though it must be hard
to see her leave for work
while he remains
to fill the empty hours
as best he may.

And will you constantly remind them both,
    Lord,
that if you number hairs on heads
and note a nestling's fall,
you know and care about their situation
and that no one
is redundant,
surplus to requirements,
not wanted any more
in your economy.

When I was prosperous, I said,
    "Nothing can stop me now!"
Your favor, O Lord, made me as secure
    as a mountain.

Then you turned away from me,
  and I was shattered.
I cried out to you, O LORD . . .
"Hear me, LORD, and have mercy on me."

Psalm 30:6–10, NLT

Is anyone crying for help?
God is listening, ready to rescue you.

If your heart is broken, you'll find God right there;
if you're kicked in the gut, he'll help you catch
your breath.

Disciples so often get into trouble;
still, God is there every time.

He's your bodyguard, shielding every bone;
not even a finger gets broken.

Psalm 34:17–20, *The Message*

Retirement

You crown the year with your bounty,
   and your carts overflow with abundance.

Psalm 65:11, NIV

All experience is an arch where through
Gleams that untravelled world, whose margin
   fades
For ever and for ever when I move.
How dull it is to pause, to make an end,
To rust unburnished, not to shine in use!
As though to breathe were life.

Alfred Lord Tennyson, *Ulysses*

Dear God, you know that we are reaching
that age and stage of life
at which the challenge of retirement
—which seemed until so recently
to be a million miles away—
looms large on our horizon.

And you know, God, that many wives
of my acquaintance
have faced this major change
with mixed emotions.
Saying that even though they may have
   married
for better or for worse,

they were not, at the time, aware,
that this included lunch!

And even while we laugh, God,
as always,
there's an element of truth
within our joking.
For while we've shared
our lives, our homes, our beds
for many years,
there's always been some space
in our togetherness,
the challenge of our work
to give us focus,
the completion of a task
to bring us joy.

And so, dear God, I bring you
   our retirement.
And ask that as you bring one season
   to a close
you'll crown these coming years
with health
and fruitfulness;
bringing into our lives
fresh challenges of faith
and opportunities for service
that we will grasp with joy.

Help us to treasure
the extra time

we have for one another;
learn to relax, and, yes,
to play again.
But in it all, please keep us free
from selfishness,
our vistas always wide,
our hearts responsive
to others' needs.
Knowing there's no retirement
from your service.

Life can become once more a grand adventure
if we will surrender it to God. . . . He brings one
adventure to an end, only to open another to
us. He is tireless and inexhaustible. With him we
must be ready for anything.

Paul Tournier

Yet Another Wedding

[Jesus said,] "The sorrow in my heart is so great that it almost crushes me. Stay here and keep watch with me." . . . He returned to the three disciples and found them asleep.

Matthew 26:38, 40, GNB

God has said,
"Never will I leave you;
   never will I forsake you."
So we say with confidence,
   "The Lord is my helper; I will not be afraid."

Hebrews 13:5–6, NIV

Why did I accept it, God?
that invitation
to yet another wedding?
As I slip into the church,
alone,
murmur congratulations—
to the bride for her beauty
and the groom for his wise choice—
deflect the questioning of aged aunts—
"No! No one special at the moment"—
my lips may smile but my heart aches,
and I just have to ask you, God,
if you have said it was not good

for man to be alone,
why am I, still, without a partner?

I'm painfully aware of all the clichés, God,
"Better to be happy and single
than miserable though married,"
so they say.
But have they ever tried to live
a single life,
when all the adult world revolves around
a tyranny of "twos"?
Where if you don't come in a pair
you are discarded,
or worse still just included
to keep the numbers right.

Please help me, God.
Help me to hang on to the fact
that I'm complete in you;
and every person you have made,
married or single,
wrestles with the melancholy monster
of loneliness
at one time or another.
For even Jesus knew this searing pain
when close friends failed
to watch and pray with Him.

And on this day, God,
help me truly to rejoice
with those who do rejoice,

and to refuse to be upset
by other people's blessings,
knowing that you will bless us all
in different ways.
And God, if marriage really is the thing
that would be best for me,
then I can trust you
that one day I will be the one
to send out invitations
to yet another wedding.

From tomorrow on I'll be unhappy,
    from tomorrow on—not today.
Today I will be glad and every day.
No matter how bitter it may be
    I'll say,
    from tomorrow on I'll be unhappy, not today.

**Written in a
concentration camp**

For the Sake of the Children

[The Lord] knows . . . you promised before God that you would be faithful. . . . "I hate divorce," says the Lord. . . . "I hate it when one of you does such a cruel thing." **Malachi 2:14, 16, GNB**

Dear Lord, I've heard today
about another marriage
breaking down.
It happens, Lord, so often in the world today,
that sometimes I am shocked,
because I am no longer shocked,
at all the cruel things that those
who once were very much in love
can say and do to one another.

But this time, Lord,
there is no obvious reason
for my friend to leave a marriage
which has survived frequent house moves,
serious illness,
a shaky business venture,
and all the normal pressures
of a family growing up.

She says that she is tired, Lord,
stifled, bored,
needs her own space,

an opportunity to be her own person
before it is too late.
And so she has convinced herself
that three teenagers
can cope
with parents splitting up
because they, too, will soon be leaving
to create futures of their own.

Please help her, Lord.
Help her to read the desperation
in her daughter's eyes,
even while she's trying to say
what her mother wants to hear.
Help her to hear the fear
that fuels the shouting match
and the refusal to do school work
from a son
whose world is threatening to crash about his
    ears.

And, Lord, help both these parents to
    understand
that children never "take it in their stride"
when marriages break down
and families break up.
So give to them the guts and grace
to find what they both need
within, rather than outside of, this relationship.
And help them rediscover love
so that they'll live together once again

with joy
and not just
for the sake of the children.

In a world that hears the deafening shrill of parents demanding their rights, it's important to hear from children, however uncomfortable that may be.

Bishop James Jones

The two Top Commandments devised by a group of teenagers:

1. You should not be allowed to get married unless you are really sure.

2. It should be illegal for parents to leave their children.

A Woman and
Her Children

A family is a mobile strung together with
invisible threads—
  delicate, easily broken at first,
  growing stronger through the years,
  in danger of being worn thin at times,
but strengthened again with special care . . .
continuity!

Thin invisible threads . . . which hold great
weights,
  but give freedom of movement—a family!
Knowing that if a thread wears thin and sags,
  there is help to be had from the Expert—the
Father
"of whom the whole family in heaven and earth
is named."

Edith Schaeffer

I'm Going to Have a Baby

Shout for joy to the Lord, all the earth....
come before him with joyful songs....
give thanks to him and praise his name.

Psalm 100:1, 2, 4, NIV

Dear God, it's true!
It's totally and definitely true!
The doctor has confirmed it,
I am going to be a mother—
we are going to be parents.
Thank you, oh thank you,
for this new life
that you have given.

My heart is singing, God,
I want to buttonhole
each stranger that I meet,
telephone my family,
burst in upon my colleagues,
and tell them
this fantastic piece of news.

Thank you for the human love, dear God,
of which this baby
is the seal and sign.
Thank you for my body
which cradles and protects our child.
Help me to care for myself

in the right way;
living sensibly, eating wisely,
enjoying the marvel of a changing shape.
Even the misery of morning sickness
and the mind-numbing fatigue
that eats into my evenings
are made more bearable
because they are the signals
of the special secret
that up to now
I've hugged within myself.
Thank you that my husband shares my joy,
  God.
That he is thrilled to think that he will be a
  father.
Thank you for his tenderness to me;
his availability
to do the extra chores,
his patience
with my up-and-down emotions,
his willingness
to listen to my fears.

For God, you know that even though
this baby has been planned,
longed for, prayed for,
that there are times
when I'm afraid.
I wonder whether I will cope
with labor and delivery.

And how I will be able
to care for all the needs
a tiny baby has.

Oh bless him God—or her.
Please make this little body grow
just as it should.
And somehow let our baby know
even within the womb
how very much it is already loved.
And in the next few months of waiting, God,
will you begin to shape us,
teach us, train us
so that from the beginning
we'll lay the right foundations
to be the kind of family
we really want to be.

When it was time for Elizabeth to have her baby,
she gave birth to a son. Her neighbors and
relatives heard that the Lord had shown her
great mercy, and they shared her joy.

Luke 1:57, NIV

Dedication

People were bringing little children to Jesus to have him touch them, but the disciples rebuked them. When Jesus saw this he was indignant. He said to them, "Let the little children come to me and do not hinder them, for the kingdom of God belongs to such as these."... And he took the children in his arms, put his hands on them and blessed them. **Mark 10:13, 14, 16, NIV**

[Hannah said,] "I prayed for this child, and the Lord has granted me what I asked of him. So now I give him to the Lord." **1 Samuel 1:27–28, NIV**

Please bless this very special day, Lord,
when we will come,
and witnessed by our family and friends,
present our child to you.
You know that we shall undertake
to do all that we can
to bring him up
to know and love you.
And Lord that is a daunting task
and one that we could never undertake
without your help.

He has received so many lovely gifts, Lord,
each one a token of the joyful welcome
that exists for him.
But will you show us, Lord,
how we can give him
those vital but invisible presents—
roots and wings,
security and freedom.
Lord, please help us to root him
in the truths of your word;
in the security of knowing
that he is totally loved,
completely accepted
and infinitely precious.
That he can depend
not just on his earthly parents alone,
but on the Maker of the universe,
the only perfect parent,
who never makes mistakes.

And then, Lord, help us to free him
to be the person
that you have created him to be.
Show us the talents
and gifts you have given him
and give us the skill
and the wisdom
to help him develop them fully.
And when the time comes for questions,
help us to give honest answers

and then stand aside and allow him
to choose for himself
whom he will serve.

As in a greenhouse certain conditions need to
be present if the delicate seedlings are to grow,
so as parents we will see our family relationships
blossom most freely if we ourselves have a deep
and growing relationship with God. God can
then work in our lives so that the qualities that
reflect his parenthood of us can gradually be
produced.

Marion Stroud[10]

Tantrums

And now a word to you parents. Don't keep on scolding and nagging your children, making them angry and resentful. Rather bring them up in the loving discipline the Lord himself approves.

Ephesians 6:4, TLB

Before we had children, most of us will have watched other parents do battle with their children, often in embarrassingly public places, and vowed we would never resort to bribing, shouting and smacking—only to fail horribly when similarly tested. **Marion Stroud[11]**

Commitment is spending two years teaching someone to walk and talk and the next eighteen to sit down and be quiet!

Dear Lord, this has been
the kind of a day
that I would like
to blot out of my memory.
So many petty irritations, Lord,
which,
when stuffed silently into my grievance sack,
one upon another,
weighed down my spirits
and shortened my patience

until I exploded
with a temper as far out of control
as the tantrum my toddler produced
in the midst of the line
at the supermarket.

I was so cross
and so tired and unreasonable, Lord,
and I took it out on my children
who are too small to understand
why suddenly their mother had become
a roaring monster.
And it wasn't their fault, dear Lord,
it really wasn't their fault.
Behavior that on a good day
would have received a gentle rebuke
was treated
like the biggest crime in the book.
Small wonder that they flew round
trying to appease,
their eyes fearful.
I cringe when I think of it, Lord,
and want to beg
their forgiveness—and yours.

It frightens me, Lord,
to think
how helpless these little ones are
in the face of adult power.
How vulnerable they are
to being unfairly treated.

Forgive me, Lord,
for failing to remember
that they, too, have their needs
and that I have a responsibility
before you
to meet them with patience and love.

I have to remind myself
that to a child
life is just as big
as it is to me.

Ulrich Shaffer

Within the family circle, it isn't just the children who have needs, parents have them too. . . . As children grow older, we may find that we judge their behavior by the way it affects us. If it stops us from meeting our own needs of the moment, then we see it as negative behavior. If it doesn't interfere with our needs, we take a far more positive view.

Marion Stroud[12]

First Day at School

Education is helping the child to realize his potentialities.

Erich Fromm

The first day at school is a major step for a five year old. Starting school is as hard as the first day at the first job and as frightening as moving to a country that speaks a different language.

Maggie Durran[13]

Father, today is *the* day—
the one that I've both dreaded
and looked forward to;
the day my youngest child starts school.

How fast the years of babyhood and preschool
have flown by, Lord—
although at times they did seem everlasting—
so that today
the door of that phase of our lives
clicks softly shut,
as she steps out
into a wider world.

Thank you that she is so keen to go, Lord.
Up and dressed before first light,
school bag packed and repacked

with an endless pile of treasures;
survival kit for this adventure
away from home.

Thank you that you can go with her
where I cannot.
Be near her in those unfamiliar rooms
filled with new faces—
and thank you for an older brother
to watch over her on the playground—
help him to be caring without being bossy,
protective but not overpowering.

Please be with her teacher
and help her to cope with so many newcomers
who have such widely differing backgrounds
and needs.
Give her the skill and patience
and the understanding to teach them,
and right from the beginning, Lord,
help my child to discover
the joy and the excitement that learning can
   impart.

Please give her friends, Lord,
but keep her close to you
as she's confronted
by different belief systems,
family values and ways of doing things.
Protect her
from physical harm and negative influences

and enable her to enjoy
all the positive things
that the first years of school can bring.

Jesus grew in wisdom and stature, and in favor
with God and men.

Luke 2:52, NIV

Encouragement

Let us... help one another to show love and to do good.... Let us encourage one another.

Hebrews 10:24, GNB

We all need what psychologists call "strokes." Positive strokes are vital for the well-being of all of us, but they are especially important for children. Essentially they are words, attitudes and actions which encourage us and make us feel good about ourselves.

I do not understand, Lord,
why often
we should find it so much easier
to correct
and criticize our children
than we do
to encourage and affirm.

Why should we be
in such a hurry to find fault
at home
within the very place
where they might hope to find a refuge
from the discouragement
so freely offered
by an uncaring world?

Please help us, Lord.
Give us the words
to say how much we love them.
The mindset
that values effort
just as much as the achievement;
the sensitivity
to notice small improvements
in attitude and action.

Thank you, Lord, for making them
with their own special blend
of gifts and graces.
And help me to remember, Lord,
those traits I find so irksome
in my children
are often those
I've yet to deal with
in myself.

One thing scientists have discovered is that
often-praised children become more intelligent
than often-blamed ones. There's a creative
element in praise.

Thomas Dreier

The atmosphere in the home can be
revolutionized when parents are on the look-out
for all they can praise in their children's words,

attitudes or actions . . . I am convinced that we need to reward, encourage and commend our children for every effort they make to do right or be co-operative.

Jean Watson[14]

Quality Time

Teach us to number our days and recognize how few they are; help us to spend them as we should. **Psalm 90:12, TLB**

If I cannot give my children a perfect mother, I can at least give them more of the one they've got.... I will take time to listen, time to play, time to be home when they arrive from school; time to counsel and encourage. **Ruth Bell Graham**

Dear Lord, please help me
to give my children time.
Time, when we are not just living our lives
side by side,
but time
when we are truly aware
of one another;
enjoying making things,
learning things
and even more difficult, Lord,
just *being*
together.

You know how very busy
our lives are, Lord.
Jobs to do, places to go,
people to see.

How many times
in every day
I look at my watch and say,
"Hurry up, we have to. . . ."
And that
in spite of all the modern machines
that are supposed to give us
more time.

Slow me down, Lord.
Help me to really grasp
that I don't have to be
a great housekeeper or an enviable cook,
giving to the school,
the community
or even the church,
if this means that my children
are left on the sidelines
and given the remnants
of my time.

You have called me to be a mother, Lord,
so please keep me from being distracted
by the many other activities
that make it so difficult
for me to enjoy my children.

And when my conscience tells me
that I should be out there
in the wider world
doing my bit for the needy,

please remind me
that I will be adding
a far greater burden
to society
than I could hope to alleviate
with all my good deeds,
if my own children
are not loved and trained
and made to understand
that they come first
with the most important people in their world—
their parents.

Every day comes just once in a lifetime. Today
you are creating tomorrow's memories. Invest
in positive memories, for childhood memories
mould the person of the future.

Marion Stroud[15]

Teach Us to Pray

One day Jesus was praying in a certain place. When he finished, one of his disciples said to him, "Lord, teach us to pray, just as John taught his disciples." He said to them, "When you pray, say: 'Father . . .'"   **Luke 11:1–2, NIV**

Fix these words of mine in your hearts and minds;... Teach them to your children, talking about them when you sit at home and when you walk along the road, when you lie down and when you get up.   **Deuteronomy 11:18–19, NIV**

You taught your disciples to pray, Lord,
responding to their request
for words
that would forge a relationship,
and enable them to live
the kind of life
that they observed
in you.

Over the years, Lord,
I too have learned
just a little
about prayer.
But there is so much, Lord,
that I still don't understand.

So many times
when I feel
that I don't pray
for the right things
or do it
in the right way.

And now, Lord, I want to teach
my children to pray.
Help them to understand
that you are someone
who knows them personally,
and loves them dearly.
Enable me to explain
that you are always with them—
without giving them the impression
that you are a frightening,
mysterious,
all-seeing schoolmaster.

And in teaching them
that they can bring their requests to you
at any time
and in any place,
keep me from giving them the idea
that prayer
is a magic wishing well.
Help us to accept
that "No" and "Wait"
are also answers.

Frameworks of prayer are useful, Lord,
so help me to choose
those that are appropriate
to a child
of this generation.
But help them also to grasp
that they can talk to you
without following
any set form or pattern,
for you are their friend
as well as their God.

Teach children how they should live, and they will
remember it all their life.

Proverbs 22:6, GNB

Help!

Don't be afraid to bring the details of your problems to God. He is never bored or impatient. He is equally ready to be involved in the small concerns that fill our hours, as He is available to help us when we are faced with major crisis management. Be definite and specific in your praying, saying to God, "This is what I need."

When Jacob was faced with a long-estranged brother who had four hundred armed men at his back, and the possibility of a blood feud being avenged, he was open about his fear of what lay ahead: "Save me, I pray, from the hand of my brother Esau, for I am afraid that he will come and attack me, and also the mothers with their children." **Genesis 32:11, NIV**

Eliezer had the responsibility of match-making for his master's son in a land in which he was a stranger, and so he made his plans—and then laid them before God: "When I came to the well today, I prayed, 'Lord, God of my master Abraham, please give me success in what I am doing. Here I am at the well. When a young woman comes out to get water, I will ask her to give me a drink of water from her jar. If she agrees and also offers to bring water for my camels, may she be the one you have chosen as the wife for my master's son.'"

Genesis 24:42–44, GNB

Dear Lord,
I ask that you will make me strong
As the holidays are six weeks long
And I don't have the wisdom or the might
To referee each and every fight
To sort out who had which thing first,
Who was best and who was worst
And who called who a nasty name
And why SHE always spoils the game.

Please give me patience infinite
When they declare they hate Marmite*
And my pantry's just been filled
With a "special offer" Marmite hill,
Or when they argue at breakfast time
Because "the cereal toy is MINE!"

Make me merciful when they hate the food I
  cook
The things I do and the way I look
And stop me from going completely nutty
When someone kicks over another potty
Or when chips and crumbs cover the floor
And a salesman's standing at the door
And the dog's barking, the phone's ringing
And someone upstairs is loudly singing
To "East 17,"* all out of tune

And a recorder's squeaking in another room
And the teakettle's broken, it's starting to rain
And they want to watch *Dumbo* all over again.

Forgive me, when in total despair
I rub their sandwiches in their hair
Because they said it wasn't fair
Not a single one willing to share
The only red plate.

Janice Fixter

Guilt Trip

Make a careful exploration of who you are and the work you have been given, and then sink yourself into that. Don't be impressed with yourself. Don't compare yourself with others. Each of you must take responsibility for doing the creative best you can with your own life.

Galatians 6:4, *The Message*

Many of us feel under pressure to be an all-singing, dancing, juggling, creative parent with a degree in the "right" way to nurture children. We can cave in under this pressure... we do not have to be talented at everything, the talents we do have are from God anyway, so let's not worry overly about the talents we were not given.　　**Sheila Bridge**[16]

You know I've felt so guilty, Lord,
because I've dared to stop to think
about the things I do not do.
I don't get up and run around the park,
greeting the dawn
and getting fit
although I'm regularly invited
by those who give this form of exercise
a high priority.

Nor am I very often on my knees
taking an hour to talk to you
before my family has stirred;
for you have given me a body clock
that takes its time to splutter into life
but then keeps going steadily
long after other folk have gone to bed.

I realize I should be reading, Lord,
keeping my mind alert
and up to date.
For sadly there's not much to be discussed
at gatherings of adults
about the antics of a railway train,
the wickedness of foxes
or rising scales of juvenile delinquency
in kittens and in rabbits!

And then there is the sewing, Lord.
I must confess that I am not the one
who volunteered to make the costumes
for the junior play;
and when it comes to knitting
I'm simply glad my children have a granny.
But when his mother drops the hint, Lord,
that husbands nowadays
do not enjoy the care and the attention
that wove the fabric of their father's lives,
I really wonder if I am scoring
any points at all.

So thank you, Lord, for your reminder
that I'm the only one who can be me.
And as myself, I'm absolutely fitted
to do the tasks
and be the wife, the mother
and most of all the person
that you intended me to be.
Amazing thought,
that without me
the sum of your creation
would truly have a gap
that simply can't be filled
by any other.

Lord, forgive our preoccupation with identity.
Keep reminding us that it is secured in you
   And that we're one of a kind,
So very special, and in a class of our own.

Jan Markel

Shopping with a Daughter

This is the day the Lord has made;
let us rejoice and be glad in it.

Psalm 118:24, NIV

Few of us will ever be able to claim
life's big prizes
but we are all eligible
for life's small pleasures.

A sparkling morning,
a kiss in passing,
that long-awaited letter,
a cup of coffee with a friend,
a bargain discovered
just when we were faced
with more month than money!
An empty parking place,
swans gliding down the river,
a great meal,
a glorious sunset.

Enjoy life's tiny delights.
There are plenty for all of us
and they come fresh-minted
every day.

Thank you, God, for this day
which I will spend

shopping with a daughter.
Thank you for the fun that it can be
to look for clothes
with someone
who actually enjoys shopping!
Thank you for this time we'll spend together.
In our talking, help us to share more
than the comparative costs,
or why
"Mary's mother" would never let her wear that!

But, Lord, you know that these outings
are not always filled
with sweetness and light.
So please help me to allow her genuine choice;
to refrain from pushing her
into buying something that she doesn't like
and that will be a source of friction between us
for ever after.

And help her to be reasonable, Lord.
To understand that our budget is limited
and that it is both unwise and unnecessary
for her to try to look
years older than she really is.
May we both feel
when we tramp home footsore
and (hopefully) heavily laden
that it has been a good day.
Come with us please, Lord,
on this special day

which I will spend
shopping with a daughter.

Hope returns when I remember
 this one thing:
The Lord's unfailing love and
mercy still continue,
Fresh as the morning, as sure
as the sunrise.

Lamentations 3:21–23, GNB

Forgive Me

Generous in love—God give grace!
Huge in mercy—wipe out my bad record....

God make a fresh start in me
    Shape a Genesis week from the chaos of
    my life
Bring me back from gray exile
    Put a fresh wind in my sails
Give me a job teaching rebels your ways
    so the lost can find their way home.

From Psalm 51, *The Message*

Dear Lord,
I've done it again!
I thought I'd got a handle on the problem;
no more nagging I promised myself,
and I really meant it.
But you know what happened last night . . .
sparked off by all the petty irritations
that grate along the surface of our lives.

Her bedroom . . . a disaster area—
even though she'd promised
to tidy it before she went—
and that shirt that I had ironed so carefully
tossed in the corner
with her wet swimming things;

it wasn't simply crumpled Lord,
it smelled!

Then there was that note from school,
hand delivered,
or I'm sure
that I would not have seen it.
Her project work,
a month behind schedule,
and yet she had assured me
that she had no homework,
knowing well enough
there'd be no evening out
if I had realized
the true state of things.
Surely she understands by now, Lord,
that education is important
if she wants a job that offers interest and
    satisfaction
as well as a paycheck
at the end of the week.

Her lateness was the final straw, Lord,
when she strolled in
just before midnight
not having phoned, when she had missed the
    bus,
so that I imagined her kidnapped, raped, or
    murdered.

She was in the wrong, Lord, but so was I,

not waiting for an explanation, but exploding,
raking up old scores
until the whole conversation became a
  confrontation,
a screaming match in which there were no
  winners,
just the deeply wounded.
All through the sleepless hours
I've been haunted by the memory of her face.
Half shocked, half scared . . .
and then that awful frozen shut-in look.
Why Lord?
Why do I keep repeating the same old
  mistakes?
I can't forgive myself
so how can I hope that she'll forgive me—
or expect you to?

My dear child . . . When I forgive, I forget.
Through Jesus' sacrifice your sin is put away
from you, and from me for ever. So when I look
at you today, I don't see you in the light of your
past sins and failures. As far as I am concerned,
those things no longer exist. It is as if they never
were.

Colin Urquhart[17]

The Prodigal

No one can persuade another to change. Each of us guards a gate of change that can only be opened from the inside. We cannot open the gate of another's will, either by argument or by emotional appeal.   **Marilyn Ferguson**

His bedroom's empty, Lord,
and he has gone.
We always knew that it would happen one
    day—
but not like this, dear Lord,
Oh! not like this.
Our dreams were all of college,
or waving him off proudly
to his first job away from home.
Not anger,
bitter words,
a backpack
crammed with hastily assembled possessions,
a slammed front door,
and silence.

What is it, Lord,
about this youngest son of ours,
that just compels him
to be so desperately
and defiantly different?

What did he see in us
to make him reject education,
a job—with or without prospects—
belonging, faith . . .
everything that we hold dear?
Where did I go wrong?

You know I fought him, Lord.
Tried to impose the discipline
he seemed incapable
of applying to himself.
I did it in love . . . and yes,
more than a little fear.
But the more I clung on,
the more he kicked and struggled.
Even now I would have argued,
    pleaded,
tried to persuade him,
to give things one more try.
But his father insisted that the time
    had come
to let him have the dignity of choice
and the responsibility
of living with the consequences of
    that choice.
And so we let him go:
dear Lord, we had to let him go.

Be with him in that "far country,"
    wherever it is.
Protect him from the evil that preys

on the vulnerable and foolish ones.
And when he thinks of home and family,
don't let pride hold him prisoner.
Remind him that the door stands open for his
   return.
And when that day comes,
help me to welcome him
with that same open-hearted and accepting
   love
that you offer—to both of us.

Marion Stroud[18]

Stop your crying
   and wipe away your tears.
All that you have done for your children
   will not go unrewarded;
they will return from the enemy's land.
There is hope for your future;
   your children will come back home.
I, the Lord, have spoken.

Jeremiah 31:16–17, GNB

A Daughter's Wedding

The greatest gift that you can offer your newly married children is to make the effort to establish a harmonious and loving relationship as parents-in-law. Hopefully you have a wisdom and maturity from which they can profit, even if you never offer advice unasked. Your uncritical support and constant encouragement can be a valued asset. No favoritism. No side-taking. Just a quiet, constant defense against the fierce and potentially destructive forces that batter every marriage.

Before so very long, Lord, we expect to be
dancing at our daughter's wedding.
And indeed, we do rejoice
that you have touched her life,
guiding her choice
to a young man who loves you,
and loves her with a quiet commitment
that bodes well for the future.
Our hearts are lifted by their happiness
and at their bright plans
for the future.

But perhaps, Lord,
only you will ever know
how much we'll miss her
as she moves so far away.

You understand
the aching sense of loss I sometimes feel
knowing that from now on
this house is not her home
and that she has new loyalties
because her husband
must now be first
in her commitment and considerations.
Bless them
as they stand together before you
making promises
that far surpass their ability
to keep
unless you help them.
Give them the love which cares enough
to put the other's happiness
before their own.
Keep them from being possessive
or jealous,
instead help them to liberate one another
to be the best that they can be,
not totally absorbed
within their own concerns
but looking outward, together,
in the same direction.

And once again, as we become
parents-in-law,
as well as in love,
help us to welcome

with uncritical hearts and open arms
this new son that you have added
to our family.

A wedding in the family
Fresh faces, new ideas
We welcome you with open arms
For you are someone special
And your coming
Adds something very precious to our lives.

Marion Stroud[19]

Entrusted to Him

The Lord will perfect that which concerneth me: thy mercy, O Lord, endureth forever: forsake not the works of thine own hands.   **Psalm 138:8, AV**

You have been speaking to me, Lord, about my children and grandchild. You loaned them to me for a season. Now I am to take my possessive, managing hands off—strictly off. You will perfect them in your way and in your timing. Years ago you began this work. It is your business to complete what you start. You have promised that you will. It's as good as done.   **Catherine Marshall**[20]

To protect them from pain.
That is what I have always wanted to do, Lord.
To shield them from the hurts
the problems and the pressures of life.
Natural enough, wouldn't you say,
for a mother to feel like that?

When they were small I could do it, Lord.
Cradle them in my arms and wipe away their tears,
bringing back the smiles
with the promise of a treat,
the assurance of my love,
even a sticking plaster* was enough
in those much simpler days.

But life is just not like that any more, Lord.
And when I see them struggle
with all the pressures
that life puts on the young these days,
especially when the problem's brought about
by traits of aptitude or character
in which I see myself,
or feel they stem
from my shortcomings as a parent,
I want to beg, "Lord, let me bear it for them:
help me to put it right."

But this is not your way, Lord.
Your loving dealings with us
allow for struggle and dark days
and living with the consequences
of our choices,
as well as laughter, joy, and happy
   endings.
So when my adult children weep,
as I have stomach-churning certainty
   they do,
they needs must do it silently,
and often they must weep alone.

And I can only watch and pray, Lord,
standing with them in unspoken trouble,
available but not intrusive,
loving but not smothering,
watchful but not inquisitive.
Praying

that the good work you have begun
   in them
will be completed
in your time and in your way.
Believing
that they can never put themselves
totally beyond your reach
and what you promise
that you will certainly
perform.

I am not ashamed, because I know whom I have
believed, and am convinced that he is able to
guard what I have entrusted to him for that day.

2 Timothy 1:12, NIV

An Arrow in His Hand

Children are a gift from the Lord . . .
The sons a man has when he is young
   are like arrows in a soldier's hand.
Happy is the man who has many
   such arrows.

Psalm 127:3–5, GNB

My daughter and her husband
have said that you have called them, Lord.
To serve you in that mighty continent of Africa,
where there is so much poverty
and suffering and pain.
The leaders of the church agree, Lord;
recognizing your guidance in my child's life.
Delighted—dare I say it—
to have their own live missionary at last.

And as the clergy organize the details,
the money needed, and the promises of prayer,
they do give me a kindly word in passing,
telling me how happy I must feel
to see my children
giving up good jobs and glowing futures,
and for your sake
serving the underprivileged members
of your family.

But you and I know Lord,
that reality
is rather different.
Of course one half of me rejoices
to see my daughter,
dedicated to you in infancy,
finding faith
and responding with such joyful readiness
to meet the needs of others
whatever it may cost.
But Lord, you also see
the tears that soak my pillow
as I wrestle with my fears for them.
Picturing a war-torn land
where disease is rampant
and transport and medical facilities
almost non-existent.
You are there, Lord,
when I ache at the loss of family togetherness,
realizing that for my grandchildren
I will be
a smiling face in a photograph
rather than a hand to hold, and arms to
    snuggle into.

Please help me, Lord,
to see this yielding of my family to you
not as loss
but as part of the harvest
that I have sown and prayed for in their lives.

Help me to encourage them, joyfully.
To pray for them, faithfully.
To see myself as part of the team
that serves you, with them.
Remembering that anything that I can give
pales into insignificance
compared with your son,
given to be impaled on a cross
for me.

"Grieve not then if your sons seem to desert you, but rejoice rather; seeing the will of God done gladly. Remember how the psalmist described children? He said that they were an heritage from the Lord, and every man should be happy when he has his quiver full of them. And what is a quiver full of but arrows? And what are arrows for but to shoot? So with the strong arms of prayer, draw back the bowstring and let the arrows fly—all of them; straight at the Enemy's hosts."

Jim Elliot, writing to his parents

Let Nothing Be Wasted

[Jesus] . . . said to his disciples, "Gather the pieces that are left over. Let nothing be wasted."

John 6:12, NIV

There was nothing left over but "broken pieces," and yet of those fragments our Lord said, "Gather them up that nothing be lost." Even so, our dear Lord cares for the broken pieces of our lives, the fragments of all we meant to do, the little we have . . . to offer, and he will use even these fragments. He will not let even the least of our little broken things be lost. **Amy Carmichael**[21]

Our failures. That's the hardest area, especially when they have affected the lives of our loved ones . . . it hurts to see areas of need and struggle in their lives that stem in part from ways we have failed them.

But even these areas are part of the "all things" which God will use to make a man and a woman who will accomplish his unique purposes. So when thoughts of failure and regret push their way into my consciousness, I let his total forgiveness dissolve my regrets, and go on to praise him who accepts us just as we are, and lovingly works to make us more than we are. **Colleen Evans**[22]

First of all face God with the problem, and then face the problem with God.

Dear God, what's happening to our family?
A few short months ago
the house was buzzing
with life and laughter.
Meal times a babble
of conversation;
the future bright
with hopes and plans.
And now, almost without warning,
everything has gone
so terribly, horribly, wrong.
What was whole and beautiful
has fallen apart
into so many separate pieces.

As I weep before you, God,
you gently remind me
of what you did
with broken lives,
splintered dreams,
shattered people,
fragmented things.
"Gather up the pieces that remain," you said.
"Let nothing be wasted."

How can I gather up the pieces
of this situation, God?
I know that there are others close to me
whose hearts are broken too,
but wouldn't come to you for help.
Perhaps, if you will comfort me
then in my turn
I will be able
to comfort them.
And maybe somewhere down the line
I'll see the point
of this experience
and have new insights
to share with others.

And in the meantime, God,
since you've allowed this pain
for some unfathomable reason,
help me not to waste it.
Help me to learn from overwhelming failure,
this leering monster
that seems to stare me in the face.
Teach me how
to be more caring for myself
as well as others
as everything within me
feels crushed
by this enormous weight.
From this day on, dear God,
to be so much more sensitive

and less dismissive
of others' pain.
For otherwise this suffering will be
a senseless futile exercise,
and that would surely be
the greatest waste of all.

The Lord hears my weeping;
   he listens to my cry for help
   and will answer my prayer.

Psalm 6:8, GNB

Joseph said to them, "Don't be afraid. . . . You
intended to harm me, but God intended it for
good, to accomplish what is now being done,
the saving of many lives."

Genesis 50:19, NIV

We know that in all things God works for the
good of those who love him.

Romans 8:28, NIV

There is no situation so chaotic that God cannot,
from that situation, create something that is
surpassingly good. He did it at creation. He did it
at the cross. He is doing it today.

Bishop Moule

On one occasion the good Lord said,
"Everything is going to be
all right." On another, "You will
see for yourself that every
sort of thing will be all right."

In these two sayings the soul
discerns various meanings. One
is that He wants us to know that not only does
He care for great
and noble things, but equally for little and small,
lowly and simple things as well. This is His
meaning: "Everything will be all right."

We are to know that the least thing will not be
forgotten.

Julian of Norwich

Child Free

I am worn out with grief;
    every night my bed is damp from
      my weeping;
    my pillow is soaked with tears.
I can hardly see;
    my eyes are so swollen.

Psalm 6:6, GNB

The . . . heart learns to recognize and to cope with the demons along the way; those elements of life that pull us into . . . darkness, discouragement, and self-pity. They can become so strong that we fall by the roadside and feel that we can never rise again. The demons which we encounter can eat away at our self-esteem, cause us to question our own goodness or the goodness of life, and create a great anxiety about the future. We lose hope of recovery, of moving on, and we think that we simply cannot do what is asked of us . . . the journey is too much for us. **Joyce Rupp**[23]

Jesus did not come to explain away suffering or remove it. He came to fill it with his presence.

Paul Claudel

I thought that I had come to terms with it, Lord.
That the pain was over,

and that I had learned to think of us
as a "child-free"
rather than a "childless" couple.
To concentrate on being a twosome
rather than a family,
and to offer you the ache in my heart
and the emptiness in my arms
whenever I peeped admiringly at a newborn,
or was caught in conversation near the school
   gates.
But today it is back,
washed in on a tidal wave
of other people's family joy.
Why did I have to meet them all
in one short hour of shopping?
Jenny—a grandmother by Christmas, she says;
Margaret, trying on that ridiculous hat
for her son's wedding;
and Christine, full of her coming visit
to her daughter and family
on the other side of the world.
And while I smiled
and congratulated them
one by one,
my heart cried out all over again,
"Why, God, why?
Why have we been excluded
from this beautiful and exclusive club called
'Parenthood'?"

For it isn't just me, you know, Lord!
My husband feels it too.
Other men have the exploits
of their children and grandchildren
with which to enliven their conversation
and brighten their leisure hours.
They may grumble about the expense
and the anxiety,
but not for a moment
would they exchange their situation for his,
however much
they might appear to envy him his freedom.

Please help me, Lord.
Deal with the hurt,
the sense of something missing
and that corroding self-pity
that sears my heart as painfully as any
  branding iron.
And please reassure me—
that there will be someone, somewhere,
who will welcome my visits
when I am old.

I know that I need to focus
on the good things that have enriched our life;
the freedom to travel
and to enjoy our friends and wider family;
the extra time we have been able to give
to nephews and nieces
who talk to us with a frankness

that would amaze their parents.
And the students who have occupied our spare
  bedroom
and filled the kitchen
with smells of exotic cooking,
widening our horizons
with their varieties of culture and belief.

Children of our own we may have lacked . . .
but never love.
Love of family, love of friends,
and most constant of all your love.
For that priceless gift which brightens the future,
and gently dispels the darkness of today,
I thank you Lord.

Marion Stroud[24]

Accepting one's life means also accepting
the sin of others which causes us suffering;
accepting their "nerves," their reactions, their
enthusiasms, and even the talents and qualities
by means of which they outshine us.

Paul Tournier

The only cure for suffering is to face it head on,
grasp it round the neck, and use it.

Mary Craig

"Sing, O barren woman,
    you who never bore a child;
burst into song, shout for joy,
    you who were never in labor;
because more are the children
    of the
    desolate woman
than of her who has a husband," says the Lord.

Isaiah 54:1, NIV

To accept the will of God never leads to the miserable feeling that it is useless to strive any more. God does not ask for the dull, weak, sleepy acquiescence of indolence. He asks for something vivid and strong. He asks for us to co-operate with him, actively willing what he wills, our only aim his glory.

Amy Carmichael

A Woman at Work

The work that I shall do today
is God's gift to me;
Whether I am working for money or for love
is irrelevant in His sight.
I can invest my energies and skills
to build things that will last
in my own life
and in the lives of others;
or I can fritter my talents away
without thought or consideration.

But the work that I do today is important
because I have exchanged a day of my life
for it.
When tomorrow comes,
today will be gone forever.
I hope that I will not regret
the return that I receive for it.

Days of Small Things

I was small among my brethren,
    and youngest in my Father's house;
I tended my Father's sheep.
My hands formed a musical instrument
    and my fingers tuned a psaltery.
And who shall tell my Lord?
The Lord himself, he himself hears.

Extra psalm from the Septuagint

May my prayer be set before you like incense; may the lifting up of my hands be like the evening sacrifice.   **Psalm 141:2, NIV**

It is almost time for bed, Lord,
and what have I to offer you
out of this ordinary day?
I have entertained a toddler
and straightened the house
after the joyful havoc
that his three-year-old energy created.

I have listened to the woes of a teenager—
and held back on the good advice—
although the solution to the situation
was staring me in the face, Lord,
it really was!
I have dispensed tea and sympathy

to an elderly neighbor,
written two letters
and made three phone calls.
Yet another load of shopping
has been selected
from the supermarket shelves,
paid for,
transported home and put away.
I have cooked dinner,
counseled a client,
written a report . . .
hardly significant in the eternal scheme of things.

And yet, Lord,
you have said that the music
made by the touch of our hands
on the lives of others,
is heard—and appreciated—
even though so often
it seems to be a silent song.
And that among all the myriad things that are
    held
in the memory of an all-seeing Father
are the little "labors of love";
all the tiny inconspicuous things
which are done in Jesus' name.

So, Lord, here is my day of small things—
an evening sacrifice
offered
with open hands and a loving heart.

God is not unjust; he will not forget your work and the love you have shown him as you have helped his people and continue to help them.

Hebrews 6:10, NIV

A Prayer for Ironing

I am glad that no line can be drawn between things that we call "sacred" and what we call "secular." What we do once in a while, or what we have to do continually—all is important to God.

Rita Snowden

Turn my whole being to your praise and service.

St. Ignatius of Loyola

Tonight, Lord, I am looking at
an overflowing mound
of ironing.
You know, Lord, that it's not a job
I hate,
but simply one
that always seems less urgent
than another—until tonight.

And now, Lord, as I sort and dampen,
smooth and fold,
instead of praying with my friends at church
help me to be aware
that you are here
and I can do this simple task
for love of you—
and of my family.

Thank you, Lord, we have so many clothes
to keep us warm,
that there is such variety
in color and in texture.
Crisp office shirts—Lord bless my husband
as he wears them.
May he feel clothed in love
as well as poly-cotton.
These well-worn tops for school—
buttons on threads,
paint-blotched, cuffs frayed,
hardly able to contain
the exuberance
of the small bodies that will fill them
tomorrow.
Lord, keep my children safe
and smooth their paths through life
as I erase the wrinkles from their clothes.

Thank you for the linen, Lord.
This tablecloth which we have bought—
a souvenir of happy holidays.
I thank you for the meal times it has graced,
a talking point for guests,
a splash of sunshine on a dismal day.
And as I fold these sheets bequeathed by
   grandparents
who've prayed so long and lovingly
for us and ours,
please wrap us in your grace

and send us into this new week
clean and attractive,
Lord, for you.

⤙⤙

Little things come daily, hourly, within our reach,
and they are not less calculated to set forward
our growth in holiness than are the greater
occasions which occur but rarely. Moreover
fidelity in trifles, and an earnest seeking to
please God in little matters, is a test of real
devotion and love. Let our aim be to please our
dear Lord perfectly in little things, and to attain a
childlike simplicity and dependence.

Jean Nicolas Grou

God does not want us to do extraordinary
things; he wants us to do the ordinary things
extraordinarily well.

Charles Gore

Food, Glorious Food

How hard it is to find a capable wife! . . . She brings home food from out-of-the-way places. . . . She gets up before daylight to prepare food for her family. **Proverbs 31:10, 14, 15, GNB**

The fulfillment of living comes from being fully focused on the present moment. At first glance it seems silly to put full attention on a task such as cooking. But that is precisely the point. When we are "mindful," a task such as cooking (and all our everyday chores) becomes part of the harvest, part of the exquisiteness of life, instead of the boredom of life. **Susan Jeffers**[25]

The office day is over, Lord,
and as I clear my desk and put aside
the tasks that have demanded my attention
throughout the last few hours,
I pause to make a list
of all the things I've yet to do
before I can relax and say
that my day's work is done.

And foremost in my mind, dear Lord, is food.
That area of life which is both pleasure
and an unrelenting grind.
All other household tasks can wait my time

and I've machines that take away the labor
of so many of them.
But there is no machine
that will both plan the meals
then shop for them and cook
and satisfy the clamor
that will greet me as I walk in through the door,
for food.
Thank you, Lord, that there is food to cook
readily available
on supermarket shelves.
Thank you for the sheer variety
from which to choose;
do help me, Lord, to make wise choices,
pleasing our palates
while nourishing our bodies
without extravagance.
And keep me always mindful, Lord,
of those who'll fall asleep tonight uneasily
with need for food unmet.

Thank you, Lord, for lessons I have learned
over the years,
in order to save time as well as money.
Give me the discipline today to plan ahead,
and find the patience
to teach and train my children
to take their part
in cooking and in washing up.

And most of all, Lord, as we gather round the
   table
please make our evening meal,
whatever we are eating,
a time when we can share our lives
as well as food;
strengthening our spirits
as much as our bodies.

Be present at our table, Lord.
Be here and everywhere adored.
This mealtime bless, and grant that we
May feast in heaven, Lord, with thee.

Each time we eat may we remember God's love.

A prayer from China

The Interview

We can make our plans but the final outcome is in God's hands.   **Proverbs 16:1, TLB**

The Spirit of Jesus often shuts doors in the long corridor of life. We pass along, trying one after another, but find that they are all locked, in order that we may enter the one he has opened for us.

Lord, this is the day
on which I have to face an interview
and I am nervous.
You know how much I want a job, Lord,
and not just any job
but this especial one
which seems so very suited
to my experience.
But in this present economic climate, Lord,
where there's more people
seeking work
than there are jobs for us to do,
there is no guarantee that I will get it.

Thank you, Lord, that I have reached
the short list;
given the opportunity to meet the boss
and show what I can do.
Please help me to find the place

and get there in good time,
wearing the right clothes.
Remind me not to talk too much Lord,
and prod me if I talk too little.
Enable me to listen carefully
and answer clearly,
presenting the skills I have to offer
effectively.

You know that I have prayed
about this job, Lord,
and whether
this is the place in which you want me
to work and witness
for you.
And so far it has seemed, Lord,
as if you've given me the green light
to proceed.

So if the job is offered, Lord,
I'll take it.
But if I'm wrong
please block the way
by shutting up this door
of opportunity.
And if this happens, Lord,
enable me to trust you
that in your perfect time
you'll lead me
to just the very job
you have in mind for me.

In everything you do, put God first, and he will direct you and crown your efforts with success.

Proverbs 3:6, TLB

Yes, Lord
Your will is my conscious choice
Nothing more
Nothing less
Nothing else.

Elisabeth Elliot

Stepping Out

The adventurous life is not one exempt from fear, but on the contrary one that is lived in full knowledge of fears of all kinds; one in which we go forward in spite of our fears.   **Paul Tournier**

Face fear with faith—and do it anyway.

And so, dear Lord,
the time has come
when I must step out
of the familiar,
the comfortable and the secure,
to face a new world
peopled by strangers,
who will perhaps expect of me
more than I feel able to perform.

You know I feel uncertain, Lord,
not unlike the Janus man,
ambivalent,
my head straining to look
both behind me and ahead,
and my anticipation
tinged
with just a little fear.

Help me to trust you, Lord,
to trust you
with my family.
Assured that with you
they will cope
with all life brings their way,
even though
I am not constantly available
to meet their needs.

Help me to trust you
with those projects
in which I have invested
a large part of my energy
thus far.
Knowing that while they still have a place
in your economy
you will provide resources needed;
and that when they come,
endings need not be seen as failure
but completion.

And help me, Lord,
to step out into the unknown with confidence,
trusting that you will never lead me
where your hand cannot cover and protect me;
and that I will never find myself
in any situation
which is beyond your grace to keep me,
or outside your power to heal.

Far better it is to dare mighty things,
to win glorious triumphs, even though checkered
by failure,
than to rank with those poor spirits
who neither enjoy much nor suffer much
because they live in the grey twilight
that knows neither victory nor defeat.

Theodore Roosevelt

Labor of Love

Whatever your hand finds to do, do it with all your might, for in the grave... there is neither working nor planning nor knowledge nor wisdom.

Ecclesiastes 9:10, NIV

Work is the natural exercise and function of a man . . . not primarily a thing one does to live, but the thing one lives to do. It . . . should be the full expression of the worker's faculties, the thing in which he finds spiritual, mental and bodily satisfaction, and the medium in which he offers himself to God.

Dorothy L. Sayers

Thank you, Lord, for giving me a job
that usually affords me
both joy and satisfaction.
Thank you for leading me
into an occupation
which stretches my mind,
expands my skills
and gives me the fulfillment
of knowing that I am doing something
that is of use
to others.

As I pause, Lord, at the beginning
of this new working day,
please bless everything
that I shall have to do in it.
Give me genuine interest
and enthusiasm
for all the tasks that I must tackle
and keep me from procrastination, Lord,
over the parts
that I find difficult
or boring.
When I am stuck for inspiration, Lord,
or find some hidden snag
in what I thought
was just a simple job,
keep me from panic
or impatience
either with myself or others.
Remind me at that moment, Lord,
that you are there
and I can always come to you for help
with no necessity
for an appointment.

Although I'm working for an earthly boss—
thank you that she is generally
a pleasure to do business with—
help me to keep in mind
that though the money which I earn is welcome,
in the end it must be you

to whom I have to give account
and it is your "well done"
I covet.

Work is love made visible.

Kalil Gibran

God has created me to do Him some definite
service; He has committed some work to me
that He has not committed to another.
I have my mission.

John Henry Newman

When love and skill work together, expect a
masterpiece.

Just for Today

Steep your life in God-reality, God-initiative, God-provisions. Don't worry about missing out. You'll find all your everyday human concerns will be met. **Matthew 6:33, *The Message***

So don't be anxious about tomorrow. God will take care of your tomorrow too. Live one day at a time. **Matthew 6:34, TLB**

What is hard by the yard is a cinch by the inch.

You know it's not my normal habit, Lord,
to live for one day at a time.
For I've supposed that setting goals
and making long-term plans
to be the better way
to keep a handle on a busy life.
And so there is a tendency
to juggle with the weeks and months ahead,
rather than to focus
all my energies upon the now.
But at the moment, Lord,
the future seems too much to grapple with,
and so I ask that you will give me what I need
to cope with life,
just for this day.

Just for today, Lord, will you please give me
    patience
to live and work in harmony with those
who seem to want to thwart me
at every turn.
And I need perseverance, Lord,
to press on with a job
I find distasteful.
Humility to help me to accept
that at the moment
it seems your place for me
is to be just a little cog
within a large machine.

And while my heart and mind are under
    pressure,
help me today
to gently tend my body,
and meet its short-term needs of sleep and
    rest
as well as exercise and food,
rather than become despairing
because I cannot tackle
all its flaws at once.

Just for today I give you my "to do" list, Lord,
and ask for help to tackle
just one thing at a time
beginning with the most important;
even if that might not appear to be
the job that's clamoring

for my attention.
Help me to stick with that task, Lord,
until it's finished,
and then move on
to do the next,
working steadily
in harmony with you,
just for today.

He said not "Thou shalt not be tempested, thou shalt not be travailed, thou shalt not be afflicted," but He said, "Thou shalt not be overcome."

Julian of Norwich

Whose Responsibility?

Children are a great comfort in your old age...
and they help you to reach it faster too!

Mothers don't have to accept the blame for their
adult children's choices. When freedom to make
their own decisions has been handed over, so has
the responsibility for the outcome of those decisions.... God has the final word on what happens
to your family.

Dear God, my daughter says
she must return to work
because they cannot pay the bills
without a second income.
And so my grandson will become
a "minded" child,
spending his days
within another woman's care,
sharing her attention
with several others.

Dear God, I find it very hard
to come to terms with this
or even start to feel
that it is right.
Although I know
such family arrangements are common

within this generation,
and alongside nurseries and child-caregivers
many grannies
are doing a second stint
of child-raising.
Please help me, God, to know
just how I should respond
and whether
you have a part for me to play
in all of this.

Help me to honor my children's right
to make their own decisions
and to support them through it.
If there must be a child-caregiver,
please lead my daughter to her
and provide
someone who'll care
for this and other little ones
with love and understanding.

And God, if you want me to offer
to take this child
and care for him for you,
even though
I have my own job, responsibilities, and needs,
help me to be obedient with joy
and see it as a privilege
to have a part in hands-on nurturing
the coming generation,
knowing

that you are no man's—or woman's—
debtor.

The women said to Naomi, "Praise the Lord!
He has given you a grandson. . . . May the boy
become famous in Israel! Your daughter-in-law
loves you. . . . And now she has given you a
grandson, who will bring new life to you." . . .
Naomi took the child, held him close and took
care of him.

Ruth 4:14–16, GNB

Just when a woman thinks her work is done . . .
she becomes a grandmother.

Reconciled

If you are offering your gift at the altar and there remember that your brother has something against you, leave your gift there in front of the altar. First go and be reconciled to your brother; then come and offer your gift. **Matthew 5:23–24, NIV**

Make every effort to live in peace.... See to it that no one misses the grace of God and that no bitter root grows up to cause trouble.

Hebrews 12:14–15, NIV

Dear God, it seems as if I have offended
a colleague.
I have both said and done something
she doesn't like
and she is angry,
hurt,
and telling everyone
but me.

Dear God, you know I didn't mean it.
I simply acted on the order
to entertain the visitor from out of town
without intending
to manipulate the situation to my advantage
or show my colleague
in an unfavorable light.

Thank you, God, for the courage
of the one who told me,
explaining why there was a sudden silence
when I walked into the room.
But then she said
I shouldn't try to put it right
or to apologize
because the injured party
wouldn't want the problem
brought out into the open.

Dear God, why is it
that we women can so often
vent our anger
by shredding one another's character
with words to others,
and then be so reluctant to make peace
with the one
we feel has wronged us?

I shudder at the thought of confrontation, God,
but neither can I work with someone
knowing
she has a grudge against me.
So will you help me?
Give me an opportunity
to see her on her own, God,
and the courage
to take it when it comes.
Help me to say the right words
lovingly,

and will you then please turn this enemy
back into a friend.

A love of reconciliation is not weakness or
cowardice. It demands courage, nobility,
generosity, sometimes heroism, an overcoming
of oneself rather than one's adversary. . . . In
reality, it is the patient, wise art of peace, of
loving, of living with one's fellows, after the
example of Christ, with a strength of heart and
mind modeled on his.

Pope Paul VI

It takes two sides to make a lasting peace, but it
only takes one to make the first step.

Edward M. Kennedy

Unwanted

It is impossible to overemphasize the immense need men have to be really listened to, to be taken seriously, to be understood.   **Paul Tournier**

Anxious hearts are very heavy, but a word of encouragement does wonders!
                                        Proverbs 12:25, TLB

Dear God, my colleague
is facing
an abortion.
She has conceived a child
who is not wanted, God,
and so the only answer seems to be
a fleeting visit
to a clinic;
a tiny life
"terminated,"
snuffed out,
almost before
it has begun.

Dear God, she's asked me
for my counsel.
What do I say, dear God,
what *do* I say?
You know that all within me

screams a veto;
for only you give life,
and you will never give
without a purpose.
But she has no belief in you
to guide her,
no faith that if you give
you will uphold.

And God, it isn't me
who's over forty;
I haven't just begun a new career.
I do not have to agonize
that this child
could be sick
or damaged,
that I might have
to bring it up
alone.

Dear God, please be there
at our meeting.
Enable me to listen
and to love.
To be the kind of sounding-board
she needs, God,
and in the tumult of emotions
and the clamor of her needs,
will you speak
words of comfort
and of hope?

But most of all, God,
will you give her
what I can never give—
the courage
to think again.

The advice of a wise man refreshes like water from a mountain spring. Those accepting it become aware of the pitfalls on ahead.

Proverbs 13:14, TLB

Well-Dressed

Let us put aside the deeds of darkness and put on the armor of light.... Clothe yourselves with the Lord Jesus Christ.

Romans 13:12, 14, NIV

I really must confess, Lord,
that armor for my spirit
is not the first thing that I look for
as I forage in my closet
for clothes to wear today.

And this is foolish, Lord,
because I know that soldiers,
or even foreign correspondents
who operate within a war zone,
would never venture out
without protective clothing,
however lacking
in style or comfort
that might be.

And what will surely govern
this day's gain or loss
will not be a designer suit
or trendy sportswear,
but the inner armor you provide
as I begin once more

the daily struggle
against the "rulers, authorities and cosmic
  powers
of this dark age."

Help me to remember, Lord,
that as I "put on Christ"
I am allowing your qualities
of love, compassion, endless patience,
and a willingness
to turn the other cheek
to garrison my heart;
and that the clothing you supply
in which to face the enemy
is woven through with praise.

So thank you, Lord,
for your provision and protection,
assuring me
that just as long as I stand firm,
face the foe head on
wearing the armor you supply,
and using the weapons you provide,
strongholds must yield,
the enemy must flee
and I need never fear what he can do
to me or mine
for Jesus has already won
the victory.

The weapons we fight with are not the weapons of the world. On the contrary, they have divine power to demolish strongholds.

2 Corinthians 10:4, NIV

Life is a hard fight, a struggle, a wrestling with the principle of evil, hand to hand, foot to foot. Every inch of the way must be disputed. The night is given us to take breath, to pray, to drink deep at the fountain of power. The day to use the strength which has been given us to go forth to work with it till the evening.

Time Trap

The days allotted to me
had all been recorded in your book
before any of them ever began.

Psalm 139:16, GNB

Your strength will equal your days.

Deuteronomy 33:25, NIV

Dear Lord, you know I start this day
facing a working mountain
that seems unscaleable.
There are so many things I need to do,
and each of them,
apparently,
a top priority.
If I could have eight hours
without an interruption
then maybe, Lord,
there'd be some hope
of getting through.

But phones will ring,
the unexpected will occur,
and doubtless colleagues will have needs
for which they will require
if not my help,
then my co-operation.

Please be here in my workplace, Lord.
Enable me to think clearly,
work quickly,
and to know
when interruptions should be heeded,
when ignored.
Keep me calm
and even-tempered,
remembering always that people matter
more than things.
And help me to be alert, Lord,
to the inner prompting of your Spirit
showing me things
that I might otherwise
overlook.
So that this evening
I may look back
and know that I have accomplished
those things which are essential
for eternity.

There are always enough hours in every day to
do the perfect will of God.

Edward Dayton

A Tibetan monk once crossed the Himalayas on foot during the Chinese occupation of his country. When asked how he managed such a difficult journey he replied: "That's simple. One step at a time."

A Woman Who Cares

Dear Lord, help me to spread Thy
   fragrance
   everywhere I go.
Flood my soul with Thy spirit and life.
Penetrate and possess my whole being
   so utterly
   that all my life may only be
      a radiance of Thine.
Shine in me and through me
   so that every soul I come into contact
   with
      may feel Thy presence in my soul.
Let them look up and see no longer me
   but only Thee, O Lord.

John Henry Newman

The Perfect Friend

The Lord would speak to Moses face to face, as a man speaks with his friend.   **Exodus 33:11, NIV**

I've loved you the way my Father has loved me. Make yourselves at home in my love.... You are my friends when you do the things I command you. I'm no longer calling you servants because servants don't understand what their master is thinking and planning. No, I've named you friends, because I've let you in on everything I've heard from the Father.
   You didn't choose me remember; I chose you.

John 15, *The Message*

Lord God, you are the perfect Friend.
Other friends may fail to rejoice with me
over small triumphs,
or hardly notice when life overwhelms me,
but you never disappoint me.
When I long for help or encouragement,
you always have the right word
for the situation.

You understand me completely.
There isn't a thought in my mind
or an intention of my heart

that you are not aware of.
I am never alone
because you are always there beside me;
neither day nor night,
distance nor circumstances
can ever separate us.
In your total knowledge
you can lead me in a path of absolute safety,
and so I can follow you
with complete confidence.

When you point out my faults
you do not accuse,
but touch the tender spots with the finger of
    love.
A love that is like the sunshine
lighting up the world on a spring morning,
dispelling the gloom of winter.
You bring joy into my life.
You are my friend.
I give you thanks and praise you, Lord.

He is a friend in need . . . so we needn't be
afraid when we have nothing to bring him but our
grief and fear. We shall be very welcome. He is a
friend for all seasons . . . however hopeless and
dark things seem.

A. B. Simpson[26]

Think of God as being all and infinitely more to us than any human friend. The one who is personally interested in us; who has made priceless sacrifices for us and is ready to take any trouble, go to any expense to help us.

Hospitality

When [the disciples] landed, they saw a fire of burning coals there with fish on it, and some bread.... Jesus said to them, "Come and have breakfast."
John 21:9, NIV

Do not forget to entertain strangers, for by so doing some people have entertained angels without knowing it.
Hebrews 13:2, NIV

Dear Lord, we are expecting visitors today.
Help me, please, to welcome them
with genuine warmth of heart
as well as central heating.
For at the tail-end of this very busy week
I really would prefer just to relax,
put my feet up,
take the easy option
in food and occupation,
instead of cooking, cleaning, coping, caring.

In spite of that, Lord,
please enable me
to order my priorities aright.
To remember that a simple meal
shared with love
is better than a banquet
laced with tension and anxiety.

Give me the grace
to accept offers of help
with a smile
and a thankful heart for their caring,
rather than a ruffled spirit
when they don't do it my way.

Where I have not got time to polish, Lord,
make our home glow
with your peace and your presence.
Please keep their eyes
from the hole in the carpet—
and those indelible crayon marks
on the paintwork—
and as we welcome these visitors,
who are newcomers
to our church and our community,
thank you that you will be our guest, too.

Though we do not have our Lord with us in
bodily presence, we have our neighbor who, for
the ends of love and loving service, is as good
as our Lord himself.

Teresa of Avila

In Webster's dictionary, the definition for
hospitable is wedged between the word
"Hospice" which is a shelter, and the word
"Hospital" which is a place of healing. Ultimately,

this is what we offer when we open our home in the true spirit of hospitality. We offer shelter; we offer healing.

Karen Burton Mains[27]

Listening and Loving

See my Servant... I have put my Spirit upon him...
He will be gentle—he will not shout nor quarrel...
He will not break the bruised reed, nor quench
the dimly burning flame... He will encourage the
fainthearted, those tempted to despair.

Isaiah 42:1–3, TLB

Should we feel at times disheartened and discour-
aged, a simple movement of heart towards God
will renew our powers. Whatever he may demand
of us, he will give us at that moment the strength
and courage that we need.

Francois de la Mothe Fénelon

Dear Lord, I've failed lamentably today
to show your love.
I listened inattentively
and spoke impatiently
to one of your beloved ones,
who is both aged and needy.

The signs were there for me to read, Lord.
The tired eyes and the slumped shoulders,
the listless movements and the toneless voice.
I should have known
that this was not the time to be cheery

or to insist on looking
on the bright side,
dismissing fears
and coming up with pat solutions.

For what she needed then, Lord,
was my time;
a hand to hold,
ears that would listen patiently
to all the cares that loomed so large
on her horizon,
and someone who'd acknowledge and accept
the way she felt
without suggesting
that she was wrong.

But I was in a hurry, Lord,
so just for once
I wanted her to see my need
for quick decisions,
a positive outlook, an encouraging word.
And when that didn't happen, Lord,
I didn't bother to curb impatience,
riding roughshod on her complaints.

I cringe to think about it now, Lord.
For when I fail those
you have placed within my care
I'm failing you.
Please change me, Lord.
Help me to honor and encourage her,

to see that I can be
enriched by her wisdom,
challenged by her courage,
and to focus always
on offering comfort, joy, and hope
in the way
that she is able to receive it,
rather than
the way that I find easiest to give.

Be at peace regarding what is said or done
in conversations; for if it is good, you have
something to praise God for, and if bad,
something in which to serve God by turning your
heart away from it.

St. Francis de Sales

The care of the old is a vocation as delicate and
difficult as the care of the young.

James Douglas

At Home Where It's Hardest

All service ranks the same with God.

Robert Browning

Many "lone" Christians long to serve God, and feel frustrated and restricted by their family situation. They forget that seventy per cent of people claim to have taken their first steps along the journey of faith through having a friend or family member to whom God is a living reality. So they have their mission field right on their door step for they have the honor of being an ambassador for God and a channel of his love to the most important people in their world—their family. **Marion Stroud**[28]

Dear Lord, why should it be
that serving you within the church
or the community
seems so much more attractive
than doing the same thing
within our own four walls?
Perhaps it is
that those who know us best
are often quick to point out gaps
between profession and performance.

Whatever the root cause may be, Lord,
teaching children about your love,

welcoming strangers,
praying for others,
serving coffee,
or even washing dishes
seems to have
a greater significance in your economy
when done at church,
or in the wider world,
than when we do
much the same thing at home.

And yet, Lord, you remind us
that you sent the man,
whose sanity you had restored,
not on a prayer vigil,
a preaching tour,
or even on a protest march
about pigs and their conditions,
but back home
to his family
to demonstrate that he was truly changed
and tell them
how much you had done for him.

God did not save you to be a sensation.
He saved you to be a servant.

John E. Hunter

Love ever gives
   forgives
     outlives
Love ever stands with open hands
   and while it lives it gives.
For this is love's prerogative
   to give
     and give
       and give
         and give.

Foot Washing

Our God... turned the curse into a blessing.

Nehemiah 13:2, NIV

You matter to the last moment of your life, and we will do all we can to help you, not only to die peacefully, but to live until you die.

Dame Cicely Saunders

One day I went to a service which was based on the theme of how the Lord washed the disciples' feet. I found myself thinking how much I would love to have the chance to wash the Lord's feet, to show Him that intimate kind of love and gratitude for all that He has done for me.

That evening, when I went home, my mother-in-law was struggling badly with the pain in her feet, and I suggested that we put them in some tepid water and applied some tender loving care and talcum powder as well. I suddenly realized that I had been given my wish. I had washed the Lord's feet.

My mother-in-law isn't at all like Jesus. She doesn't even know Him yet and I had been really resentful and resistant to the idea of having her to live with us. But the Lord said that if we do loving things to the least of these His brothers we have done it to Him, and a great wave of love and gratitude came over me for the Lord and for my often difficult charge. **Jennifer Rees Larcombe**

Dear God,
you know that there are times
when within me
the promised fruit of your own Spirit
seems to be
in very short supply.
For there are days when I just don't feel
loving, joyful, peaceful,
patient, kind, or good.
When faithfulness applied
to this unwanted task
seems to be the last thing
I can pray for.
And gentleness in voice and action
as far beyond my reach
as heaven itself.

Dear God, please help me.
Help me to understand
how it must feel
to be so totally dependent
upon another's care.
Enable me to see the inner person
within the aging shell,
who is still infinitely precious,
totally loved,
and absolutely accepted
by you.
And as I seek to give him

respect for who he is,
and dignity of choice,
above all else,
enable me to love him, Lord,
for Jesus' sake.

One cares for a little child for what he will become. One cares for the aged, for what they have been.

Heart to Heart

Congenial conversation—what a pleasure!
The right word at the right time—beautiful!

Proverbs 15:23, *The Message*

I loved the talk, the laughter, the sharing of the study of books... the companionship that was sometimes serious and sometimes hilariously nonsensical, the differences of opinion that left no more bad feeling than if a man were disagreeing with his own self, the rare disputes that simply seasoned the normal consensus of agreement.

Augustine of Hippo

Thank you, Lord, for this bright day
which I have spent
just talking
to a friend.
Thank you that although our homes
are now so many miles apart,
our lives lived out in different situations,
there's still that unity of heart and mind
that time has failed to weary
and absence does not dull.

Thank you, Lord,
for bringing us together
so many years ago

when tiny children dogged our steps;
for even then our friendship kept
our vision bright, and spurred us on
to pray and serve
within the limits of home-based demands.

And as our borders widened
and life's pressures grew
till sometimes they would seem
beyond our power to bear alone,
that listening ear
and ever-present willingness to stand
shoulder to shoulder
has been your gift.

And once again today, Lord,
as we face
change and transition in our lives,
we've had the chance to share our doubts,
our questions and our longings;
admit our failings and our fears,
knowing that in this "place of safety"
we are completely free
to lay aside the masks
and to explore,
without apology,
the darkness and the light contained
within the gifts and graces you have given.

Thank you, Lord, for this bright day
that I have spent

just talking
with a friend.
For in our meeting you were there,
your love was woven through our laughter
and our listening,
lifting our hearts, lightening our steps,
enlarging our faith and expectation
as we travel onward
toward you.

Jonathan went to David at Horesh and helped him find strength in God. "Don't be afraid," he said.

1 Samuel 23:16–17, NIV

Spending time with a listening friend is like a hug that lasts all day.

Reunion

I thank my God every time I remember you. In all my prayers for all of you, I always pray with joy.... God can testify how I long for all of you with the affection of Christ Jesus.

Philippians 1:3, 8, NIV

Together! What a beautiful word that is, Lord.
Somehow it holds with it
the joy,
the comfort,
the quiet security
and the sheer fun and excitement
that we have experienced this weekend.

You have blessed us with many friends, Lord.
But out of a host of acquaintances
and a smaller number of closer friends,
there are these rare and special ones
with whom our hearts
feel joyfully and totally at home.

Thank you that after all these years
we have been able to spend time with two of
   them;
and that neither time nor distance
has touched the love,
the understanding

and the indescribable sense
of belonging to each other
that binds us together as your children.

Thank you that there was no strangeness
at our meeting, no reserve;
just a gentle slipping back
into the comfortable closeness
that is such a special thing
about this particular relationship.

Thank you, Lord,
for the laughter
and the lively discussions—
we don't have to agree on every point
in order to keep our friendship intact!

Thank you for the sharing and the caring
that runs so deep.
And thank you that at the end of the day
we could join hands and pray,
bringing our joys and anxieties to you,
who has given us
this precious gift of friendship.

No woman is an island and no continents can
separate people of like mind.

Kathy Keay[29]

Streetwise

[Jesus] took a little child... in his arms [and] said, "Whoever welcomes one of these little children in my name welcomes me... And if anyone causes one of these little ones... to sin, it would be better for him to be thrown into the sea with a large millstone tied around his neck."   **Mark 9:37, 42, NIV**

Dear God, a child is missing
and no one seems to care.
They say that she is "streetwise,"
whatever that may mean;
implying that at eight years old
she can care for herself.
And that there's nothing to be gained
by headlines in the paper,
tearful interviews
with grieving relatives,
long lines of anxious citizens
searching every nook and cranny
of grimy city streets.

Dear God, she's eight years old
and "streetwise";
a friend of the homeless and of tramps they
    say.
Not often at school,
father in prison,

mother doing the best she can
with four children
in a small apartment.
And while the social workers
make hollow noises of concern,
it is implied that this child
is born to trouble,
and that in some mysterious way
she isn't really worth the worry
and allocation of scarce resources.

Dear God, forgive them.
And forgive me.
Forgive me that I can sleep at night
once I am assured
that my children are safe,
protected, loved, and cared for.
I dump the problem of all the "streetwise" ones
on someone else's shoulders,
because the pain of thinking
of little children
who have more firsthand knowledge
of crime and poverty,
abuse and fear
than I have experienced in a lifetime
seems too much to bear.

Dear God, the problem is too big
for me to handle.
All I have to offer is my availability.
But if I'm willing,

perhaps together we can make a difference.
Please make the world a kinder, better place
for just one "streetwise" child
through me.

Remove the chains of oppression and the yoke
of injustice, and let the oppressed go free. Share
your food with the hungry and open your homes
to the homeless poor. Give clothes to those who
have nothing to wear, and do not refuse to help
your own relatives.

Isaiah 58:6, GNB

After Chemotherapy

An intruder has been drip-fed into my body
   and ransacked the house of my mind.
Everything of value, or beauty, or use
   has been stolen....
What the intruder didn't think worth the taking
   I don't want either.

Shirley Vickers

In today's society we live in what can be called a death-denying culture... even when the dying individual is not physically alone, it is unusual for anyone to be with him, sensing and sharing his feelings of pain, bewilderment, and anger. If the individual tries to share his feelings, he runs the risk of being totally alone, for few people will really listen to him; fewer still will give him a meaningful response.

Ruth Kopp[30]

Dear God, my friend has just been having
chemotherapy,
and at the moment, God,
the treatment seems to be
far worse
than the disease,
if that is possible.

Please help her, God.
Help her with the sickness
and the falling hair.
Help her to hang on to you
in faith,
especially in the dawn hours
when, she says,
fear grips her by the throat.

And please help me.
Help me to listen;
to listen with my heart
as well as with my ears.
To hear the words that lie unspoken
and to try to understand
the way she really feels.

Help me to remember
that it isn't vital
to have wise words
or instantaneous
solutions.
That what she may need more
is my unsaid permission
to spew her anger out,
let her doubtings show
and find available
two loving human arms
in which to weep.

Oh, that I might learn diligently to trust him in the winter months of my soul as I do in the springtime.

Peggy Gustafson

I'm absolutely convinced that nothing—nothing living or dead, angelic or demonic, today or tomorrow, high or low, thinkable or unthinkable—absolutely nothing can get between us and God's love, because of the way that Jesus our Master has embraced us.

Romans 8:38–39,
The Message

You Did It for Me

When the son of Man comes as King . . . all the nations will be gathered before him.... Then . . . he will put the righteous people on his right and . . . will say, . . . "Come and possess the kingdom which has been prepared for you.... I was hungry and you fed me, thirsty and you gave me a drink; I was a stranger and you received me in your homes, naked and you clothed me; I was sick and you took care of me, in prison and you visited me."

The righteous will then answer him, "When, Lord, did we ever see you hungry . . . thirsty . . . a stranger . . . naked . . . sick . . . or in prison?"

The King will reply, "I tell you, whenever you did this for one of the least important of these followers of mine, you did it for me!"

Matthew 25:31–40, GNB

Dear God,
please bless the young woman
that I saw in town this morning.
You know the one—
Pale-faced, holes in her jeans,
broken-down buggy and the baby.
Oh! Why do all the beggars seem to have a
 baby—

or a dog?
Helpless, dependent creatures
which tear at my heart
as I avert my eyes
from the paper cup held out,
and try not to hear the plaintive refrain,
"Can you spare some change, please?"

Those in authority say,
"Don't encourage them. Don't give
   them money."
And perhaps in some instances
it would be spent on substances
   that damage
rather than heal body and soul.
But, God, I could have stopped,
asked her about herself,
offered to buy her a hot drink, a meal,
or some necessity—for the baby.
I'm sure that you would not have walked by
—as I did—on the other side.

Of course I can rake up so many reasons
why today was not the time
to cast aside the shackles of convention,
self-interest,
and—I must admit it, Lord—
downright fear of getting into something
that I might not be able
to handle or control.
"I was in a hurry,"

"I had to get back to work,"
and "What would my friends think
if they saw me talking to a beggar
in a doorway?"

Dear God, forgive me,
and bless her.
Give her food and warmth and shelter tonight.
And next time, give me the grace
to be a channel of your love
to these wounded ones—with or without a
  baby.

Giving is a joy if we do it in the right spirit. It all
depends on whether we think of it as "What can
I spare?" or "What can I share?"

Esther York Burgholder

A Woman Growing Older

If we accept our added years
with grace and insight,
aging can be as natural and normal
as the changing of the seasons.
We are meant to develop
one day and one year at a time,
taking with us the best of every age.
If we can do that,
age will no longer be our enemy.
It will be our guide.

Herb Montgomery

Changing Scenes

Do not cling to events of the past
    or dwell on what happened long ago.
Watch for the new thing I am going to do.
    It is happening already—you can see it
    now!
I will make a road through the wilderness
    and give you streams of water there.

Isaiah 43:18–19, GNB

Dear God, I feel as if I'm wandering around
in no man's land;
from what I've heard about the First World War,
a perilous place to be.
I've left behind so much
that is familiar, tried, and trusted
about my path so far,
and yet it seems
the next stage of my life,
when I will have a good idea
of what I'm doing,
where I'm going and with whom,
is like a mirage,
always moving
just when I think I have it
in my grasp.

It's very tempting, God, to emulate Lot's wife

and keep my focus
on that which lies behind me.
Clinging tightly to the happiness,
   achievements,
and the people in my past;
refusing to acknowledge
that it is part of life's rich pattern
that relationships,
lifestyles and goals
will change with changing years
as well as my appearance.

It's hard to be in limbo, God.
To let the old life die
before I've got the new one
firmly in my grasp.
But during this transition time
help me to be content
to wait for you,
knowing that emptiness
is necessary
if you're to have the space
to fill my life again.

The future sometimes looks a little frightening,
   God.
Thank you that there's no path
I'll need to tread
without your company.
And that in all the changing scenes of life
one thing is sure—

as you were yesterday, so will you be today and always.

You knew much of what you needed to know for what you were, but what you are going to become will require new skills and new understandings.

William Bridges[31]

I am the Lord, and I do not change. And so you . . . are not yet completely lost.

Malachi 3:6, GNB

Seasons of Life

There is a time for everything, and a season for every activity under heaven.... He has made everything beautiful in its time. He has also set eternity in the hearts of men.

Ecclesiastes 3:1, 11, NIV

Everything that happens in this world happens at the time God chooses.... He has set the right time for everything.   **Ecclesiastes 3: 1, 11, GNB**

Thank you, God, for this season of my life.
Thank you for the freedom to enjoy it.
Thank you that the slackening
of the demands of home life
mean that I can enjoy being part
of the working world once more.
Thank you for the new friends
and the fresh experiences
that have come into my life
because of it.

I'm grateful, too, for the time I can spend with
   my husband.
For the fact that we can have conversations,
without battling against crying babies,
arguing children,
or music played at full volume.

Thank you that we still have so many things
to talk about!
Thank you, too, for grown-up children
who are living their own lives
and yet still want to be part of ours.
For grandchildren who dance into our house
and fill it with joy,
but whose broken nights,
tantrums,
and school problems
are the main responsibility of
    someone else.

There are days, of course,
on which I forget to be thankful.
Occasions when I covet
my daughter's fresh prettiness
and the physical energy of
    younger friends.
When I long for the fun
of being at the center of a growing family
    once again.
Sometimes, God, you know I *do* wish
that I could turn the clock back;
that I hanker after what might have been.

At those moments, remind me about
    the pressures
as well as the privileges
of being younger.
Help me to be supportive and sympathetic

to those who are experiencing them.
Teach me to treasure this season
that you have brought me to,
which brings fresh opportunities
to live and love and laugh.
And time to learn more about myself,
those around me
and my God.

A woman's life may be framed by days and weeks and weeks and years, but it is also marked by seasons. And most of those seasons are inextricably linked with the lives of those with whom she lives and for whom she cares.

Legacy of Love

A good man leaves an inheritance for his children's children.　　　　**Proverbs 13:22, NIV**

Be very careful never to forget what you have seen God doing for you. May his miracles have a deep and permanent effect on your lives! Tell your children and your grandchildren about the glorious miracles he did. Tell them especially about the day you stood before the Lord ... and the Lord spoke to you.　　　　**Deuteronomy 4:9, 12, TLB**

Dear God, it is the hardest thing
to take apart the fabric of another's life
when they have gone to be with you.
Sorting through possessions
which were acquired
at such a cost
and now form just the shell
of an existence,
to be bequeathed or discarded or simply
　bagged
till someone can be found
who wants them.

It makes me ask myself, dear God,
what kind of legacy
I want to leave behind

for future generations.
Of course it will be good if I am able
to give them lovely things
that they will treasure,
or money that will help
to meet their needs.
But all these things will one day
wear out, rust out, or run out.
So help me please to see how I can make
investments that will last a lifetime
and beyond.

First, God, I'd like to leave behind me for
    my family
a spirit of adventure
that will see them always open
to challenge and to growth.
I'd give them a delight in your created world
and a willingness
to care for and respect it.
I'd will them insight to avoid the traps
of plastic entertainment and of shrink-wrapped
    living
so that they'd take the time to nourish
those creative gifts
with which you've blessed them.

Then if I could, dear God, I would bequeath
    them love
and that determination to be available
to one another and to those in need;

and last, but most of all,
within our wider family to form
a place of refuge where your truth
is clearly taught, believed, and then lived out
in time and in eternity.

A life devoted to things is a
dead life, a stump;
a God-shaped life is a
flourishing tree.

Proverbs 11:28,
The Message

My sword I give to him who shall succeed me in
my pilgrimage, and my courage and skill to him
who can get it. My marks and scars I carry with
me as a sign that I have fought his Battles who will
now be my Rewarder. So he passed over and all
the trumpets sounded for him on the other side.

John Bunyan

Elijah said to Elisha, "Tell me, what can I do for
you before I am taken from you?"
"Let me inherit a double portion of your spirit,"
Elisha replied.

2 Kings 2:9, NIV

Comfort Zones

The pressures of life seem perfectly calculated to harden our spirits and our minds into the safety of the known. The same prayers . . . the same system, the same joke, the same seat in church, the same friends, the same solutions to the same problems. We are free and the door is open, but how often we stay in the cage!

Dr. Richard Kriegbaum

Jesus... went up a hill... and began to teach:... "You have heard that people were told in the past.... But now I tell you ..."

Matthew 5:1, 21, GNB

Today, if you hear his voice, do not harden your hearts.　　　　　　　　　　　**Psalm 95:7–8, NIV**

I come to you with heavy heart today, Lord,
because I have been learning
some things about myself
of which I am ashamed.
I, who within myself,
have often
criticized others
for their reluctance
to move out and move on,

I, too, have comfort zones
which are like prison walls,
and yet of which, till now,
I have been largely unaware.

Long-term guests have shown me, Lord,
how loath I am
to really share my home and life
with others;
who have a different body clock,
whose tastes in food
I inwardly deplore,
who never, ever, watch the programs
I enjoy on television.

Such little things have crept
   like iron
into my soul, Lord.
I'd never thought that my routine
was so important to me
until it had to change.
I hadn't realized, Lord, how much
life's little comforts
had become a prop,
the loss of which
provoked a real rebellion
   deep inside.

Please help me, Lord.
You know that I would loathe to be
one of those

whose mind and spirit hardens
with their arteries.
I don't want to become so full of myself
that there is no room for your Spirit;
so set in my ways
that I am no longer useable, moldable,
   shapeable.
And if this means
I have to take some sweeping steps,
I'm ready, Lord—I think!

It is never too late to give up your prejudices.

Henry David Thoreau

Do not conform yourselves to the standards of
this world, but let God transform you inwardly by
a complete change of your mind.

Romans 12:2, GNB

Keep Me at It

Write to Laodicea . . . "I know you inside and out and find little to my liking. You're not cold, you're not hot—far better to be either cold or hot! You're stale. You're stagnant. You make me want to vomit . . . The people I love, I call to account— prod and correct and guide so that they'll live at their best. Up on your feet then! About face! Run after God!" **Revelation 3:14–19, *The Message***

The only thing necessary for the triumph of evil is for good men to do nothing. **Edmund Burke**

Lord, you know that there are times these days
when the energy required
to lever myself up off the sidelines
and get involved with life again
seems sadly lacking.

On those occasions, Lord, I really wonder
whether the gifts and abilities
I thought I had
can really count for much
in your economy.
And if there's any purpose
in swimming against the tide
of others' "good" advice
in order to begin again.

Lord, please help me
to fight against the torrents of discouragement,
the love of ease,
the grave temptation to take the level path.
Lord, keep me at it.
Keep me from believing the subtle lie
that as one person I can't change the world.
I know that's true Lord,
but it is also true
that with your help
I can change the world
for one person.

And when life all around me
seems confusing
and your guidance
about the next step seems so long
   in coming
that I begin to doubt
that you have ever spoken in the
   first place,
Lord, keep me at it.
Light a beacon on the mountain
that faces me
and help me to keep putting
one foot in front of the other.

Lord, keep me at it
because you know my heart's desire
is neither to rust out
nor to wear out

but to end my days and stand before you burning and shining still.

The trouble with most of us isn't active or deliberate wickedness; it's lethargy, absence of caring, lack of involvement in life. To keep our bodies comfortable and well fed and entertained seems to be all that matters. . . . We no longer hear the distant trumpet and go towards it; we listen to the pipes of Pan and fall asleep.

Arthur Gordon[32]

God save us from hot heads who would lead us foolishly and from cold feet that would keep us from adventuring at all.

Peter Marshall

Fear Not the Lions

Do not be afraid.... The Lord your God carried you, as a father carries his son, all the way you went until you reached this place.

Deuteronomy 1:29, 31, NIV

The porter at the lodge, whose name was Watchful, perceiving Christian made a halt as if he would go back, cried unto him saying "Is thy strength so small? FEAR NOT THE LIONS FOR THEY ARE CHAINED and are placed there for the trial of faith, where it is and for the discovery of those who had none. Keep in the midst of the path and no hurt shall come to thee." **John Bunyan**

Lord, you know that there are wakeful hours
when sleep eludes me,
and worries prowl around my mind
menacing,
waiting for an opportunity to pounce,
as fear-inducing
as a pride of hunting lions.

On those occasions, Lord,
the focus of my fears
is very often thoughts of getting older,
which isn't too surprising

as years pass
and I see friends,
with just a few more years behind them,
grappling with all the problems
increasing age can hold.

There is so much
that I must thank you for, dear Lord.
Good health, a happy marriage,
a quiverful of loving children,
and all the joys
that grandparenting can bring.
But Lord, however would I cope
if I should lose
this wonderful life partner
who's also my best friend?
What if I have to face a lengthy illness,
no longer able
to cope with independent living,
and worst of all, dear Lord,
if I became confused?

Forgive me, Lord.
For when I bring these fears into the light
I feel ashamed that
I've allowed them to linger.
I must be realistic
and face the fact
that they could all come true,
but you could also call me home to meet with
    you tomorrow.

And so I only have to cope
with one day at a time,
knowing that just as you have cared
for me and mine so far,
I can depend on strength sufficient for the day,
however long or short
my life may be.

Listen to me . . . you whom I have upheld since you
were conceived,
and have carried since your birth.
Even to your old age and gray hairs I am he,
I am he who will sustain you.
I have made you and I will carry you;
I will sustain you and I will rescue you.

Isaiah 46:3–4, NIV

'Tis Jesus the first and the last,
Whose spirit will see us
safe home.
We'll praise Him for all that
is past,
And trust Him for all that's
to come.

Bereavement

When Jesus saw her weeping, and the Jews who had come along with her also weeping, he was deeply moved in spirit and troubled.... Jesus wept.   **John 11:33, 35, NIV**

Dear Lord, how ever will I face my life
without the one I love?
In those last days,
when he was in such pain,
I almost prayed for his release.
But now I'd gladly have him back,
for then at least
there'd still be something I could do for him
to show how much I care.

My friends are very kind, dear Lord,
and for their thoughtfulness,
of course, I'm thankful.
The members of my family
are like a tower of strength,
but they, too, have their grief to bear,
their individual lives to lead,
and in the end
I know that every one of us
must face our loss alone.

Alone, so very much alone,
and yet I thank you, Lord,
that you are here.
No weariness or heaviness of heart,
no other duties or commitments
will take you from my side.
And I can pour my heart out to you
without the fear of adding to your pain
of being tedious
or self-indulgent.
If I could not rely on you for comfort
I don't know what I'd do.

But you *are* here
with arms outstretched
to cradle and support.
Help me to lean on you, dear Lord,
knowing that you will give me strength
not for the months or years ahead—
I cannot bear to think that far—
but for this day,
this hour, this minute.

And give me just a candle-glow of light, Lord,
within my darkness,
so I can see the next step I must take.
Oh, help me to believe that in your wisdom
you'll lead me on with gentleness
into a life that's still worth living,
however different it may be.

Other people can comfort and console us in our grief. They can be part of the healing, but only after all the waves of mourning have washed through our lives. Comfort can come only after we can accept death as a reality . . . and only as Jesus brings us to the realization that physical death is not the end.

Colleen Evans[33]

Death is not the extinguishing of the light—it is the putting out of the lamp because the dawn has come.

Rabindranath Tagore

Burning Still

John was a lamp that burned and gave light.

John 5:35, NIV
(Jesus speaking of John the Baptist in prison)

There were times, Lord,
when she seemed to have
so little going for her.
Times when we were tempted to say,
"Surely she has suffered enough."

First it was her sight
dimming, losing clarity and focus,
until all she could distinguish
were faint shapes in a twilight world.
And books, which once had given her
such joy and stimulation,
gave place to tapes
of someone else's choosing.

And then the fall,
which stole her mobility
and, worse still, her confidence.
Exchanging familiar cane
for walking frame;
unwanted badge of age and unsure steps.

But limited sight and restricted mobility
were as nothing
compared to failing memory, Lord.
For those of us who watched,
powerless to help her,
it hurt so much to see her
anxious and frustrated.
The same questions,
over and over,
as she struggled
to keep her world in focus.

And yet, Lord,
even within the prison bars
that physical and mental frailty
had forged for her,
she shone.
Uncomplaining,
grateful for every small service,
always concerned about the needs of others.

When she held her neighbor's hand,
comforting his tearfulness with old hymns
sung word-perfect and without
   embarrassment,
her light shone as it had always done,
pointing others to you,
whom she has served life-long.

And now, Lord,
you have set her free.

Her vision is restored
so that she sees you face to face.
Her body is made new
so that she can worship you
with every fiber of her being.
Her light is not snuffed out
but burns ever brighter
in the greater light of your presence.

So we thank you, Lord,
for every memory of her.
And as she has joined the great company of
    witnesses,
please let your peace and joy
comfort our hearts,
lighten our darkness,
and shine through us to others
at the end of the day.

Death has been swallowed up in victory. . . .
Thanks be to God! He gives us the victory
through our Lord Jesus Christ.

1 Corinthians 15:54, 57, NIV

Enlarge My Borders

If I had my life to live over, I would start barefoot earlier in the spring and stay that way later in the fall. I would go to more dances. I would ride more merry-go-rounds. I would pick more daisies.

Nadine Starr, age eighty-five

I will never be old. . . . To me old age is always fifteen years older than I am. **Bernard Baruch**

Thank you, Lord,
for the new freedoms
that come to me
with this stage of my life.
I am excited to discover
that letting go
need not leave me
empty or bereft,
but simply makes room
for other things.

So as I shed
the structures of the past,
fill me with lightness in my spirit, Lord,
as this new me
gradually emerges
from the chrysalis

of all that's happened
in my life so far.

Enable me to reach out and grow.
Show me the ways
in which I can expand my life,
my interests,
my capacity for loving,
for serving others,
and for knowing you.
Extend my borders, Lord,
and bring me
to a spacious place within
however limited
my physical surroundings may become.

And Lord, as you expand my borders,
will you increase the fun factor?
Help me to see the funny side
of petty irritations;
keep me walking joyfully
on the sunny side of the street
rather than stumbling along in the shadows.
Make me fun to be with
and keep my enthusiasm for life new-minted.
Remind me that I can still be
a cheerful giver
as well as a gracious receiver
and that ahead of me
lies "joy unspeakable and full of glory."

For that and for your own dear self
I thank you, Lord.

O God, save me from being
  a dull grey person,
  and let the colors of your
  creation pattern my life
  with your beauty.

Kathy Keay[34]

None are so old as those who have outlived
enthusiasm.

Henry David Thoreau

Glossary

Keeping Sunday Special

Car boot sales—used items sold out of the trunk of an automobile.

Communication Gap and Not Wanted Any More

Redundancy—to be made redundant means to be laid off or out of work.

Help!

Marmite—a dark brown-colored savory spread that has a very strong, slightly salty flavor. It is definitely a love-it-or-hate-it type of food. Children in Britain are generally fed it from the time they are weaned, and most never grow out of it. It has a high B-vitamin content, as well as riboflavin and niacin—and as such is very healthy.

"East 17"—a British pop boy band.

Entrusted to Him

A sticking plaster—an adhesive bandage strip.

Notes

1. Porter, Mark, *The Time of Your Life* (Victor Books/ Scripture Press, 1983).
2. Extract taken from the song "To Be in Your Presence" by Noel Richards. Copyright © 1991 Kingsway's Thankyou Music, P.O. Box 75, Eastbourne, East Sussex, BN23 6NW, UK. Used by kind permission of Kingsway's Thankyou Music.
3. Carmichael, Amy, *Edges of His Ways* (SPCK: London, 1970).
4. Pantry, John © 1991, Kingsway's Thankyou Music, P.O. Box 75, Eastbourne, East Sussex BN23 6NW.
5. MacDonald, Gordon, *Ordering Your Private World* (Highland Books: Crowborough, 1985).
6. Stroud, Marion, *Loving God but Still Loving You* (Scripture Press).
7. Keay, Kathy, *Dancing on Mountains* (Marshall Pickering, 1996).
8. Davis, Linda, *How to Be the Happy Wife of an Unsaved Husband* (Whitaker House).
9. Stroud, Marion, *Gift of Marriage* (Lion: Oxford, 1982).
10. Stroud, Marion, *The Journey Parents Make* (CPAS, 1994).
11. Ibid.
12. Ibid.
13. Durran, Maggie, *Understanding Children* (Marshall Pickering, 1987).
14. Watson, Jean, *Happy Families* (Hodder & Stoughton: London 1983).
15. Stroud, Marion, *The Gift of a Child* (Lion: Oxford, 1982).

16. Bridge, Sheila, *The Art of Imperfect Parenting* (Hodder & Stoughton: London, 1995).
17. Urquhart, Colin, *My Dear Child* (Hodder & Stoughton: London, 1990).
18. Stroud, Marion, *The Gift of a Child* [adapted] (Lion: Oxford, 1982).
19. Stroud, Marion, *Our Family* (Lion: Oxford, 1987).
20. Marshall, Catherine, *Light in My Darkest Night* (Hodder & Stoughton: London, 1990).
21. Carmichael, Amy, *Edges of His Ways* (SPCK: London, 1970).
22. Evans, Colleen, *Prodigals and Those Who Love Them* (Ruth Graham).
23. Rupp, Joyce, *Praying Our Goodbyes* (Eagle, 1995).
24. Stroud, Marion, *Gift of Years* (Lion: Oxford, 1984).
25. Jeffers, Susan, *End the Struggle and Dance with Life* (Hodder & Stoughton: London, 1996).
26. Simpson, A. B., *The Prayer Adventure* (Highland Books: Crowborough, 1989).
27. Burton Mains, Karen, *Open Heart, Open Home* (Cook, 1976).
28. Stroud, Marion, *Loving God but Still Loving You* (Scripture Press).
29. Keay, Kathy, *Tapestry of Voices* (SPCK: London, 1993).
30. Kopp, Ruth, *Encounter with Terminal Illness* (Lion: Oxford, 1981).
31. Bridges, William, *Transitions* (Addison Wesley, 1980).
32. Gordon, Arthur, *A Touch of Wonder* (Fleming Revell, 1974).
33. Evans, Colleen, *Give Us This Day Our Daily Bread* (Doubleday, 1981).
34. Keay, Kathy, *Dancing on Mountains* (Marshall Pickering, 1996).

Bibliography

Baruch, Bernard, *The Time of Your Life* (Winstone Press, 1977).

Bauer, Fred, *For Rainy Mondays and Other Dry Spells* (Prometheus Press, 1973).

Elliot, Elisabeth, *A Slow and Certain Light* (Word Books).

Engstrom, Ted, *A Time for Commitment* (Kingsway: Eastbourne, 1988).

Flecker, James, *The Golden Journey to Samarkand*

Foster, Richard, *Celebration of Discipline* (Hodder & Stoughton: London, 1980).

Frost, Robert, "Stopping by Woods on a Snowy Evening," *Selected Poems* (Penguin: London, 1980).

Keller, Helen, quoted in Keay, Kathy, *Dancing on Mountains* (Marshall Pickering, 1996).

Montgomery, Herb, *The Time of Your Life* (Winston Press, 1977).

McCandlish, Phillips, quoted in Simpson, A. B., *The Prayer Adventure* (Highland Books: Crowborough, 1989).

Powell, John, *Why Am I Afraid to Tell You Who I Am?* (Thomas More, 1995).

Schaeffer, Edith, *What Is a Family?* (Hodder & Stoughton: London, 1975).

Schaffer, Ulrich, *For the Love of Children* (Lion: Oxford).

Trobisch, Walter, *I Married You* (IVP, 1992).

Note to the Reader

The publisher invites you to share your response to the message of this book by writing Discovery House Publishers, PO Box 3566, Grand Rapids, MI 49501, USA. For information about other Discovery House books, music, videos, or DVDs, contact us at the same address or call 1-800-653-8333. Find us on the Internet at www.dhp.org or send e-mail to books@dhp.org.